This book belongs to:

_____

D1532703

it's a BREAKUP not a BREAKDOWN WORKBOOK

A 21-Day Action Plan
to Plot Your Revenge, Spoil Yourself, and Find Out How Good Your Life Is Without Him

lisa **steadman,** author of *It's a Breakup, Not a Breakdown*

POLKA DOT
press®

avon, massachusetts

Copyright © 2009 by Lisa Steadman
All rights reserved.
This book, or parts thereof, may not be reproduced in any
form without permission from the publisher; exceptions are
made for brief excerpts used in published reviews.

Published by Polka Dot Press, an imprint of
Adams Media, a division of F+W Media, Inc.
57 Littlefield Street, Avon, MA 02322. U.S.A.
www.adamsmedia.com

The Polka Dot Press® name and logo design are
registered trademarks of F+W Media, Inc.

ISBN 10: 1-59869-917-2
ISBN 13: 978-1-59869-917-3

Printed in the United States of America.

J I H G F E D C B A

Library of Congress Cataloging-in-Publication Data
is available from the publisher.

This publication is designed to provide accurate and authoritative information with regard to
the subject matter covered. It is sold with the understanding that the publisher is not engaged
in rendering legal, accounting, or other professional advice. If legal advice or other expert
assistance is required, the services of a competent professional person should be sought.
—From a *Declaration of Principles* jointly adopted by a Committee of the
American Bar Association and a Committee of Publishers and Associations

Many of the designations used by manufacturers and sellers to distinguish their product are
claimed as trademarks. Where those designations appear in this book and Adams Media was
aware of a trademark claim, the designations have been printed with initial capital letters.

This book is available at quantity discounts for bulk purchases.
For information, please call 1-800-289-0963.

To the breakup survivors & thrivers of the world,

Whether you know it or not, your brilliant and beautiful future still exists. Together, we WILL rediscover it.

I wish you much happiness & healing!

acknowledgments

Writing my first book was a dream coming true. Being offered the opportunity to write a second book has been just as dreamy. And I couldn't have done it without so many incredible and amazing people. Special thanks to everyone at Adams for their hard work and dedication, especially my awesome editors Jennifer Kushnier (I miss you!!!) and Paula Munier, publicist extraordinaire Beth Gissinger and her team, the ever-patient Chris Duffy, designer Colleen Cunningham for my beautiful first book, and everyone behind the scenes who makes this process magical for me. Major kudos to my agent Sharlene Martin. Thanks for being on my team and never settling for less than the best. It's a pleasure working with you! Massive thanks to the incredible members of Ladies Who Launch, who have shown that together, we can do anything! To all of my dear friends who have loved, supported, and cheered me through both tears and triumphs over the years. I love you all. I'm especially grateful to my biggest cheerleaders, Lani Voivod, Gretchen de Castellane, Scott Connell, Chris Varaste, Mattie Stevens, Melanie Hanson, and my newest sole sistahs Cindy and Karalee.

Of course, the loudest and proudest cheering section would be my family. Mom, Dad, Sissy, thank you so much for all you do to love, celebrate, and share in my Woo-hoo! journey. I love you and I'm so happy that you're my family.

Speaking of family, none of this would have been as easy or fun without the newest member of my family, my husband, Luis. You are my greatest gift, my best friend, my rock, *plus* you rock my world. I love you! Here's to our ongoing adventure together. . . .

To my other new family members, Rosa, Rosie, Jose. I look forward to a lifetime of happy memories.

And to my *other* new family members. Paul and Robin, words cannot express my thanks, love, and joy for the most unforgettable day of my life.

Judy, your kindness and generosity greatly contributed to my most magical day. Thank you all for everything you did and continue to do to celebrate Luis and me.

While writing books has afforded me many unforgettable career opportunities, it has also taken me on a spiritual journey of sorts. Along the way I have had the pleasure of working with many amazing teachers, healers, and guides. With love and gratitude, I acknowledge and thank Barbara De Angelis, Ti Caine, and Dharshan for your incredible love, energy, and gifts.

For anyone who has ever shared their breakup story with me, and for all the clients I continue to work with. I wish you much happiness and healing!

And finally, to all the Mr. Exes I've loved and lost. Thank you for the amazing memories, the life lessons, and for those of you who've contacted me since the first book came out, thank you for the closure. And don't worry. I don't name names in this book either.

contents

introduction

If you've picked up this book, you're probably going through a breakup. Congratulations! Whether you know it now or not, it's a good thing. In fact, it's an amazing, empowering, life-altering thing. I'll tell you why in a minute. But, first things first, let me ask you a question—and since it's just between you and me, be completely honest in your answer, okay?

Are you still in contact with your ex?

Are you calling, e-mailing, texting, or in any other way trying to stay connected to him?

Worse, are you still sleeping with your ex?

Or, are you a total rock star and completely avoiding him? If so, congrats! You're well on your way to healing and moving on.

But back to those of you who are still in contact with your ex. You rock too. You just don't know it yet. I'd like to help you get there. In the meantime, I've got another question for you. . . .

How is staying connected to your ex working out?

Chances are, not very well. At least, not for you. The truth is, after a breakup the single, most important factor in healing and moving on is to create distance from your ex. If at all possible, you need to cut off all communication. However, if you have kids, work together, or have other financial or business reasons to stay connected, it's essential to create new boundaries.

Not ready to let go just yet?

Trust me on this one. I know what I'm talking about. See, after my Big Breakup, I tried to stay connected. We worked together, which meant we still had to see each other every day following the breakup. Truthfully, we committed some cardinal breakup sins that you, too, may be committing. We tried to nurture each other through the breakup. We even fell in and out of each other's beds off and on for an entire year following the breakup. And then one day, I found a picture of someone new. While I had been busy holding on to Mr. Ex for dear life, he had been getting busy with someone else. Ouch!

As I said, when it comes to breakups, I know what I'm talking about.

And it's not just personal experience. On my website *www.BreakupChronicles .com* I hear from thousands of men and women who all say the same thing—breaking up is hard to do, *especially* when you hold on to your ex. After my first book, *It's a Breakup, Not a Breakdown*, came out in 2007, I heard from thousands more who all agreed that creating distance from their ex was difficult but essential to their recovery.

Recovery's a funny word, isn't it? However, if you have recently gone through a breakup, that's exactly where you are right now—in recovery. The good news is that like the millions of breakup survivors who've come before you, you will get through this. You will not only survive the pain and anguish, but will eventually thrive. You may even say *Thank God!* I know I did.

Believe it or not, breaking up kind of rocks. Not at first. Especially not when you've just been dumped out of the blue, are still in the pin-pricking voodoo doll stage, and/or when you're curled up in the fetal position wearing your ex's old T-shirt and bawling your eyes out. That part's not so fun. But after that: When you start noticing that your heart hurts a little less. When a beautiful day is not just a vicious reminder that the world doesn't care about your breakup. When, eventually, you summon the strength to pull yourself out of your slump and awaken to your most authentic self. That's when your breakup starts rocking. It's also when amazing new opportunities start coming your way. You discover your own resilience. And, as time goes on, you fall in love with life again. Possibly, you fall in love again, too.

Isn't that fantastic?

In the throes of a bad breakup, I know it's all too easy to forget that your future can still be fabulous. I'm here to tell you that your chances of *happily ever after* didn't leave with your ex. There is so much more joy, happiness, and love waiting to come into your life. But first, you've got to get through your recovery. And that's where this book comes in.

According to conventional wisdom, it takes twenty-one days to form a new habit. That's just three weeks out of your entire life. If you start reading this book today, and commit to reading one chapter a day for the next twenty-one days (don't worry—they're short chapters!), think of where you can be three weeks from now.

Are you up to the challenge?

If not, what are you waiting for? A second chance with your ex, more proof that he's not right for you, or some other form of false hope that the breakup didn't just change everything, including your future plans? Whether you know it or not, you still have a bright and beautiful future ahead of you. In order to get there, you've got to let go of your ex. I want to help you do that.

Please let me help.

It is my absolute pleasure to introduce you to this interactive twenty-one-day recovery program. In just three weeks, you can kick-start the healing process and ease into Movin' On mode. You'll learn how to mourn the loss of your relationship without losing yourself, how to cut your ex out of your life for good, and how to move on with style, sass, and class! Not only that—I've got daily tips and worksheets that'll make the healing process even easier, including nightly activities that'll keep you from dialing your ex's digits in a moment of panic.

Now, that doesn't mean your breakup recovery will be easy. In fact, some of it may be downright gut wrenching. But there will also be times when you'll feel inspired, when you'll experience a sense of empowerment, and you may even have a little fun along the way. In just three short weeks, you're going to make amazing progress. That's not to say you'll be completely over your ex in twenty-one days. But if you do the work, put in the time, and give it your very best effort, you'll be well on your way to your fab future.

Let me ask you again. Are you up for the challenge? I hope so!

This is my wish for you. Over the next twenty-one days, I wish you courage, commitment, and self-care. By being courageous, you'll resist the temptation to reach out to your ex, which is only detrimental to your recovery. By being committed, you will make remarkable progress regardless of any setbacks you incur on any given day. And, by being kind and nurturing to yourself, you'll emerge a stronger, more confident individual at the end of this journey. In just twenty-one days, you'll be that much closer to getting over your ex and moving on with your beautiful, amazing, wonderful life.

Remember, you're not embarking on this adventure alone. This is a journey we'll be taking together. A journey I have already been on, have helped so many others through, and am now honored to guide you through. If you let me, I'll take you to a better place in your life. A place where one day in the not-too-distant future, you'll be able to look back at your breakup and say, once again, *Thank God!*

Ready to get started? (I hope the answer is yes!)

Before You Get Started . . .

Before embarking on your twenty-one-day recovery program, you'll want to have the following survival supplies on hand:

1. A calendar to chart your daily progress (there is also a recovery challenge calendar on page 198)
2. Gold star stickers (like the ones you got in grade school)
3. A red Sharpie marker
4. A journal to record your progress and/or to do the daily worksheets

PLUS . . .

Sign Up for Cyber-Support

Want to rock your recovery? For additional support during the next twenty-one days, visit *www.LisaSteadman.com/breakupcoach*. There, you can get free breakup survival tips, tools, and strategies e-mailed to you every day for the next twenty-one days. Go ahead and do that now. Then keep reading.

DAY 1
throw a
pity party for ONE

Today, I feel . . .

_____

_____

_____

Congratulations for being brave and bold and putting your recovery needs first. And welcome to the first day of the rest of your amazing life! I know it may not seem like it right now, but there's a whole world waiting for you now that you're 170+ pounds lighter without your ex. A world that celebrates you and the amazing individual you're becoming, thanks to the breakup. Don't worry—you don't have to make the world a better place today. You don't even have to feel fabulous yet. Still, it's important to know that when you're ready to emerge from your self-imposed cocoon, the world will be waiting to welcome you. Until then, let's have ourselves a good old-fashioned pity party!

A word of caution before we get started. . . .

Over the next twenty-one days, you'll most likely experience every emotion under the sun: some good (relieved, happy, empowered), some bad (angry, depressed, sad), and some just downright ugly (irrational, hormonal, homicidal). Before you start your day, take your emotional pulse and jot down how you feel on these pages. Then give yourself permission to feel every emotion without judgment. There is no right or wrong way to feel during your breakup recovery. But, in order to get through the pain, you have to *feel* it. Today's no exception. In fact, today may be brutal. There will most likely be moments during the day (or night) when you'll want to give up. Times when you'd rather throw in the towel, pick up the phone, and call your ex than deal with the painful memory left in his absence (and in your bed). But you know what? You're not going to do that. And even if you do, you'll come back to this book after the regret wears off. See, you're stronger than you think. You picked up this book in the first place, didn't you? That means you've got more resilience than you know. It also means you're strong enough not only to survive your breakup, but to actually thrive without Mr. Ex.

How?

By taking one step at a time, one day at a time, and starting with your pity party.

Pity-Party-for-One Essentials

1. Call in sick.
2. Put on your most comfy clothes (It's even okay if you want to wear your ex's T-shirt that still smells like him. However, a cute new pair of PJs is a better idea!).
3. Stock up on the following supplies: tissues, comfort food, a snuggly blanket or quilt, and appropriate moody music and movies.

The Breakup Survivor's Guide to Getting Out of Work

In order to have the ultimate pity party, you need to be in a safe environment free from the watchful (and judgmental) gaze of others. That means you're calling in sick today. And because your office probably doesn't offer any breakup recovery days, the following excuses should do the trick:

If you're a little bit dramatic . . .

"(Cough, sniffle) Looks like I caught that bug that's been going around. If I rest today, I should be better in the morning (sneeze)."

If you've already run out of sick days . . .

"I think I have food poisoning. You really don't want me to come in."

If your boss is a man . . .

"It's not so much the cramps that are keeping me from coming to work today, but the raging PMS that makes me a danger to others." (No further questions necessary!)

If your boss has a sense of humor . . .

"The voices in my head are all telling me to stay home. They say I'll be better tomorrow."

If you believe honesty is the best policy . . .

"I'm having an allergic reaction to my breakup. I'm pretty sure it's just a twenty-four-hour virus."

By taking a mental health day on Day 1 of your breakup recovery, you give yourself permission to enjoy a proper pity party in style. So, once you've called in sick, turn off that cell phone, get comfy on the couch or in bed, wrap yourself in that snuggly blanket or quilt, and let the pity party begin!

Breakup Bravo!

Your boss may not be sympathetic about your breakup, but in Japan, Tokyo-based cosmetics marketing firm Hime & Company offers its female employees breakup leave. You heard me—breakup leave!

Company CEO Miki Hiradate says, "Not everyone needs to take maternity leave but with heartbreak, everyone needs time off, just like when you get sick."

Amen to that! Hime & Company gives employees under the age of 24 one breakup recovery day per year. After 25, they're entitled to two days off annually, and after 30, they get a full three days off.

"Women in their twenties can find their next love quickly, but it's tougher for women in their thirties, and their breakups tend to be more serious," Hiradate explains.

It's about time breakup survivors get the same perks as other women in the workplace! And while it's not as substantial as maternity leave, it's a step in the right direction.

Suggested Pity-Party Activities

One of the most challenging aspects of breakup recovery is the fact that suddenly you have all this free time on your hands. Time you used to spend with Mr. Ex. Time that you are now inclined to spend obsessing about Mr. Ex—what went wrong, what he's doing now, the many ways his life is going to be amazing without you while you'll most likely shrivel up and die without him . . .

Sound familiar? Oh yes, we've all been there. But guess what? I have good news. You are *not* going to just shrivel up and die without your ex. You've just committed to healing and moving on, haven't you? That means your life may get a little rocky over the next few weeks, but as time goes on (and you're patient with your progress), you're going to survive and thrive on your own. In order to get there, you need to find healthy, happy, empowering ways to fill all that free time you now have. Over the course of your twenty-one-day recovery, I'm going to give you lots of tips, tasks, and tools that'll help you heal and move on. For now, all you need to focus on is filling your pity party with the proper activities, including the following:

Have a Good Cry

Maybe you haven't stopped crying since the breakup happened. Or maybe you've been fighting back the tears because you think your ex doesn't deserve any more of your emotional energy. You know what? This isn't about your ex. This is about you and your recovery. The truth is, nothing's going to get you closer to healing and moving on than a good old-fashioned bawling session. So go ahead—let the waterworks begin! And don't even bother with the waterproof mascara today. Get messy! Cry for all the stupid things your ex ever did, for all the many ways he disappointed you, and even for all the wonderful ways you loved him. Cry because it's over, because what could have been will

never be, and because, even if you don't believe it right this very second, you both did your very best to make the relationship work.

Just when you think you've exhausted all of your energy, with your puffy eyes, and sniffly nose, cry a little more. It may not be the last time you cry over your breakup, but it's the first step in your twenty-one-day plan to get over your man.

Watch Appropriately Moody Movies

Of course, no pity party is complete without a mopey movie or two. If you're in the mood to curl up on the couch and watch something sappy (or happy!), the following flicks should do the trick:

The Breakup You'll laugh, you'll cry, plus you'll be reminded that at least your breakup didn't happen in the public eye (and your man didn't leave you for Angelina Jolie)!

Bridget Jones Diary Sure, breaking up sucks, but if Bridget Jones can survive and eventually thrive with style and sass, so can you.

Eternal Sunshine of the Spotless Mind While it would be so much easier to erase the memory of your ex after a breakup, the truth is you can't. This movie will remind you why that's a good thing.

The First Wives Club Girl power conquers all in this story of jilted wives who seek revenge!

Forgetting Sarah Marshall Here's proof that men go through breakups and actually feel pain, too. The movie's pretty funny (and features full-frontal male nudity), so you'll laugh, you'll cry, plus you'll see some actor's junk.

High Fidelity Another great film about what guys (in this case, John Cusack) go through after a breakup. This one includes a fantastic breakup soundtrack, too (more on that later).

The Holiday A fun flick about two single gals (Cameron Diaz and Kate Winslet) who, sick of their disastrous dating lives, swap homes and ultimately find love in unlikely places.

The Notebook When was the last time you cried for two hours straight? Oh wait. Never mind. On the bright side, Ryan Gosling is just hot enough in this movie to make you forget your ex ever existed.

Out of Africa Full of angst, longing, and unhappy endings. Plus, Robert Redford looks super-sexy and just might distract you from your ex.

The Way We Were The ultimate story about incompatible individuals who try to make a relationship work (sound familiar?). You'll laugh, you'll cry, and, I hope that you'll be so smitten with Robert Redford (again) that you'll forget about that silly ex of yours.

Add a few of your favorites to the list:

_____

_____

_____

10 Songs to Put into Your Pity-Party Playlist

For the perfect mix of anger, bitterness, angst, and empowerment, load your iPod with these Pity-Party classics:

1. *Before He Cheats* by Carrie Underwood
2. *How Do I Live* by LeAnn Rimes
3. *I Can't Make You Love Me* by Bonnie Raitt
4. *I Will Survive* by Gloria Gaynor
5. *Irreplaceable* by Beyoncé
6. *Killing Me Softly* by Roberta Flack
7. *Not Gon' Cry* by Mary J. Blige
8. *Nothing Compares to You* by Sinead O'Connor
9. *These Boots Are Made for Walking* by Nancy Sinatra
10. *You Oughta Know* by Alanis Morissette

Make Your Own Pity-Party Playlist:

_____

_____

_____

_____

_____

_____

_____

_____

_____

Perform an Ex-orcism

One of the most important activities you can engage in on Day 1 of your breakup recovery is to ex-orcise your ex from your home. That means getting rid of any evidence that your ex actually existed. Maybe you feel as though you're not ready yet, but this is an important and necessary step to your recovery. So wrap that comfy blanket or quilt around you, keep a handful of tissues in one hand, and with the other grab a sturdy bag or box. Now, go from room to room, putting anything into the box/bag that your ex left behind. This includes his old stuff (socks, toothbrush, Xbox, etc.), items that will only remind you of your ex and therefore torture you (old photos, letters, mementos), or gifts that he gave you (including the teddy bear on your bed). Once you've done a clean sweep of your home, clearing any visual reminders of your ex, put the bag/box down. You now have a decision to make.

1. Will you trash his stuff?
2. Are you going to donate his belongings?
3. Would you rather return the items of value, and dump the rest?
4. Or would you rather put everything somewhere for safekeeping until the end of your three-week plan to get over your man, and then decide what to do with it?

While I'm a big believer that time plus distance equals moving on, I have my sentimental side, too. I recognize that you may want to keep certain mementos from your relationship: old photos, letters, cards. However, for the duration of your three-week recovery, your ex's things have got to go! That's what the box is for. Once you've packed up all of his stuff and gotten rid of as much of it as you're willing to, close the lid on the items you want to keep. Put the box on the very top shelf of your hall closet, in a storage area you don't frequent, or better yet, give it to a friend for safekeeping. Explain that you'll eventually want the box back, but first, your heart needs to heal.

 SETBACK ALERT

If you decide to keep certain mementos, it's crucial that you hold yourself accountable for your actions. That means no rifling through the box's contents at 2 A.M., no snuggling with the stuffed animal he gave you, and absolutely no reading old letters, e-mails, or text messages during this twenty-one day healing process. Trust me, it will only lead to unnecessary tears, possibly a regrettable phone call, potentially followed by a breakup-blundering booty call. That's why it's much better to give the box to a trusted friend for safekeeping until you've sufficiently healed.

The Angry Girl's Guide to Getting Rid of Her Ex's Stuff

Let's face it. Some breakups are brutal! If you're going through such a breakup, let me suggest some ways to ditch your ex's stuff while ex-orcising your anger:

1. Throw an ex-boyfriend bonfire (be sure to have a fire extinguisher handy!).
2. Toss all of his belongings out the nearest window (first, check for pedestrians below).
3. Hold an ex-bf yard sale.
4. Put your ex's stuff on eBay along with the scathing details of the breakup.

Write Your Ex a Letter

Chances are, you have a lot of unanswered questions right now. You may even be craving closure. But don't pick up that phone and call your ex. Instead, write him a letter. Make it as scathing, saucy, and vindictive as possible. If he broke up with you, tell him all the reasons you were about to break up with him (even if it's not true). If you broke up with him but now want him back, use the letter as a reminder of why he's such a loser (even if you don't think he really is) and why you're better off without him. This is your chance to go off on your ex, calling him every name in the book, even getting downright nasty. Don't worry—you're not going to send the letter. This is just for you, so let the mudslinging begin!

Not sure how to get started? The following salutations should inspire you:

To the Jerk Formerly Known as <u>INSERT NAME</u>,

Dear Asshole,

Hey, Mama's Boy,

Yo, Shit for Brains,

To the Scumbag Who Broke My Heart,

Write your own salutations:

_____

_____

_____

_____

_____

If that doesn't get your pen flying, the following sentences should help kick-start your creativity:

You don't know the first thing about satisfying a woman and you never will!

Real men don't <u>FILL IN THE BLANK</u> (pick their nose, leave skid marks in their undies, forget anniversaries, etc.).

In case I never mentioned it, size does matter and you just weren't a good fit.

I never liked <u>FILL IN THE BLANK</u> (your friends, your job, your family, your jokes, etc.).

Great news! Thanks to the breakup, I never have to fake an orgasm again.

Did that help? Write some of your own ideas:

_____

_____

_____

_____

_____

_____

Are the ideas flowing now? I hope so. Even though you're in the middle of a pity party, you can still have some fun. If you feel like laughing, laugh! If you feel like cursing your ex out loud as you write, curse away! If you still need to cry, bawl your eyes out! The goal in writing your letter is to release any pain, angst, bitterness, and other emotions you're feeling onto the paper. Remember, you're not actually going to send the letter so feel free to unleash your inner demons and emotionally pummel your ex to smithereens!

After you've gotten all that juicy angst down on paper, you'll want to end your letter on a diva-rrific note. Feel free to adopt any of the following closing lines:

> *The next time you see me, I'll be thinner, richer, and happier. You'll still be a jerk.*

> *Thanks for setting me free. You did me the biggest favor of my life!*

> *I don't know what I ever saw in you—and now I don't have to figure it out.*

> *My friends were right. You're a total loser.*

> *If I never see you again, I'll be the luckiest girl on earth.*

Now write some of your own closing lines:

_____

_____

_____

_____

_____

Once you've finished the letter, sign it, fold it, and put it in an envelope. Then put it somewhere that's out of sight and out of mind for safekeeping (i.e. under your bed, in your dresser drawer, in that box in the closet). One day, you may want to revisit the letter, but for now, the act of writing it is what's most important.

 SETBACK ALERT:

Right about now, are you thinking of sending the letter to your ex? DON'T DO IT. While the act of writing the letter was therapeutic, sending it will only set you back in terms of your recovery. Plus, your ex doesn't need any ammunition to use against you later on. What's done is done. Put the letter away for safekeeping and enjoy the rest of your pity party.

Chapter *Check-In*

Congratulations! You just made it through the first day of your twenty-one-day plan to get over your man. Do you know how incredibly strong and brave you are? The answer is *very*! And while you may not feel like it, you *are* making progress. However, it's important to note that probably the hardest part of Day 1 is what comes next, Night 1. Nighttime is tricky. It reminds us that we're alone (especially if we lived with our ex) and that can feel scary, lonely, and isolating. It can make us question our sanity and worry about our future. But guess what? Your future is amazingly bright. If you don't believe it, you'll just have to take my word for it—for now.

Here's what I want you to do. At the end of each chapter, there's a check in. Save it for bedtime. Each night, I'll give you end-of-day tasks, meditations, affirmations, and so on, to help make being alone a little easier. Together, we *will* heal and move on. Sound good? Great!

When you're ready for bed, go into your bedroom and pull back the covers. Get into bed, and instead of sticking to your usual side, get comfy smack-dab in the center. Spread out like a starfish and take up as much room as humanly possible. Instead of focusing on the fact that he isn't beside you, place your attention on how comfortable it feels lying in the center of your bed in what is probably a new position. Don't fight the scary emotions if they pop up. Let them wash over you (but don't act on those urges to dial your ex's digits!). Tell yourself that everything will feel better in the morning. For now, you need your rest.

Your meditation for Day 1 is this: Take a few deep breaths and come up with **some reasons for why it's good your ex is gone.**

_____

_____

_____

_____

Then come up with **some reasons for why you rock without your ex.**

_____

_____

_____

_____

Even if you think your fabulousness left with *what's his name* (trust me, it didn't!), go through this exercise. This will, I hope, help ease you into a comfortable night's sleep on your own.

One last thing. Did you avoid any and all contact with your ex today? If so, congrats! Give yourself a gold star on your recovery challenge calendar. If not, circle the day on your calendar in red (we need these big, glaring visual reminders). Shoot for a gold-star day tomorrow!

worksheet 1
write your ex a letter

If you didn't already, now's the time to write that scathing and saucy letter to your ex. Make it as cruel, critical, and crazy as you like. Don't worry about sparing anyone's feelings—you're not sending the letter. So go ahead, channel all that inner angst onto the page. You'll feel better.

To better track your breakup recovery, be sure to include the date.

Store the letter somewhere safe so you can revisit it at a later date.

DATE _____

_____

_____

_____

_____

_____

_____

_____

_____

_____

_____

_____

worksheet 1
write your ex a letter—continued

_____

_____

_____

_____

_____

_____

_____

_____

_____

_____

_____

_____

_____

_____

_____

_____

_____

_____

_____

_____

worksheet 2
go to the dark place

It's perfectly okay if you're missing your ex right now. It means you're processing your pain in honest and healthy ways. To help you ease into Day 2, spend a few minutes with your deep dark thoughts. Write down how much you miss your ex, why you still love him, and why right now it feels as if your life is over without him, as your mood dictates.

DATE _____

_____

_____

_____

_____

_____

_____

_____

_____

_____

_____

worksheet 2
go to the dark place—*continued*

_____

_____

_____

_____

_____

_____

_____

_____

_____

_____

_____

_____

_____

_____

_____

_____

_____

worksheet 3
find the light

After you've visited that dark and scary side of your brain, it's time to find the light. Spend a few minutes thinking about all the ways your life is going to be a million times better now that your ex is out of it. As your mood dictates, write whatever comes up for you.

DATE _____

_____

_____

_____

_____

_____

_____

_____

_____

_____

_____

_____

_____

_____

_____

_____

_____

_____

_____

_____

_____

_____

_____

_____

_____

_____

_____

_____

_____

DAY 2
live in denial
for a day

Today, I feel . . .

_____

_____

_____

Wouldn't it be great if, after a breakup, your ex ceased to exist? Life would be so much easier if you could just press a button, and miraculously, he was ejected from the planet, his name erased from your memory, and all proof of the time you spent together disappeared. There would be no heartbreak, no explaining to friends and family what happened, no awkward run-ins with each other on dates with other people (the worst!). Although scientists have yet to develop the technology, today you get to live out the fantasy that your ex no longer exists. First, you get to decide what fantastical fate befell him.

1. Did he suffer an excruciatingly painful demise at the mercy of ravenous piranhas?
2. Was he miniaturized and shot into space in an irretrievable capsule?
3. Did he lose his head at the ex-boyfriend guillotine?
4. Or was he the victim of spontaneous combustion (It could happen!)?

Or is there some other sinister fate that he deserves more? Trash compactor mishap, food allergy fiasco, skydiving splat? It's your fantasy—you decide. But don't waste too much of your precious time thinking about your ex. After all, he doesn't actually exist today. Matter of fact, what ex? (Get the picture? Ex-cellent!)

The good news is that since you're no longer mourning the end of a relationship that never happened, you're free to have a fun and fabulous day. Sure, you should probably show up for work (unless it's a weekend, of course), but that doesn't mean your day has to be a drag. Matter of fact, slip into your fave ensemble (the one that makes you feel über-confident), spend a few extra minutes on your hair and makeup, make a quick stop for your oh-so-indulgent latte fix, and stroll into work with a spring in your step. If you happen to turn a few heads along the way, so be it. You're a total rock star and deserve all the attention and adoration that comes your way!

And because you're such a rock star, you're going to do a kick-ass job at work today, approaching every project with energy, enthusiasm, and A+ effort. Your coworkers will most likely take notice of the new and improved you (maybe the boss will, too!). They may even ask what your newfound success secret is. Simply smile, shrug, and keep on strutting your stuff, Rock Star!

Making a small change to your morning routine today can do wonders for your mood, not to mention help you enjoy your day without focusing on your ex.

Just because you have to report for work doesn't mean you can't enjoy some well-deserved "me" time during the day. Rather than eating lunch at your desk, make a point to get outside, or at least out of the office. Do not just dash out, grab some greasy fast food, and stuff your pretty face on the way back to work. Today you're going to treat yourself to something special. Whether it's a leisurely lunch at your favorite restaurant or a picnic in a local park is up to you. Just do something relaxing with a touch of decadence (that means chocolate!). Yes, you're far too fab to go without that delicious chocolate cupcake or scrumptious scoop of Chocolate Fudge Brownie ice cream today. Go ahead—indulge! You should even give yourself permission to stroll into that afternoon meeting a little late. With a satisfied smirk on your face, nobody will dare ask any questions.

BREAKUP RECOVERY TIP

℞ ### Start a New Morning Ritual

To help kick-start your day in denial, mix up your morning routine. That way, you're not tempted to think about the things you and *what's his name* used to do in the A.M. together. Incorporate these new morning rituals or add your own:

1. Set your alarm an hour early and go for a brisk walk or jog around your neighborhood before showering and getting ready for work.
2. While you're getting ready for work, instead of watching the TV news, put on some music you haven't heard in a while (that doesn't remind you of your ex), and get your morning groove on.
3. Instead of brewing a pot of coffee, steep some hot and delicious tea, pour it into a travel mug, and sip it slowly and peacefully on the way to work.
4. Change the route you take to the office, paying attention to the new sights and sounds all around you.
5. Rather than listen to the car radio, slip in a book on CD or inspirational music and enjoy.
6. _____
   _____
7. _____
   _____

SETBACK ALERT

At some point during the day, memories of your ex might surface. As liberating as a day in denial can be, the painful memory of *what's his name* may creep into your consciousness. If that happens, don't beat yourself up. Instead, take a few deep breaths, let yourself feel whatever emotions arise, and remind yourself that this, too, will pass. If you need a good cry, find the nearest private place (your car, a bathroom stall, your office with the door closed) and shed those tears. Then pick yourself up, dust yourself off, and get back to being a diva in denial!

Suggested Day-in-Denial Activities

After a long, hard day in denial, a girl's gotta do what a girl's gotta do—pamper herself! May I suggest some soothing activities to fill your evening?

Get a Manicure-Pedicure

Nothing lifts a gal's spirits quite like reclining in a vibrating chair, flipping through celeb gossip magazines, and getting her nails done. Phone a friend to join you at the salon or chat on the phone for added fun! If it's too cold outside to wear strappy sandals, wait till you get home to dance around, showing off your pretty painted toes.

Go Shopping

A couple hours of retail therapy does the diva in denial a whole lot of good! And even though *what's his name* doesn't exist today, you'll still want to purchase a new pair of cute and comfy pajamas he'll never see you in. Or maybe a sexy new bra and panty set, a saucy little black dress, or a new pair of sky-high stilettos will be your fashion fix. Even if you're on a budget, pick up something extra special today. You may be spending the day in denial, but you don't have to deny yourself a little pampering (nor do you have to break the bank to do it!).

Get a Massage

Are memories of your ex slipping into your consciousness? A relaxing massage will help knead away any and all thoughts of the jerk formerly known as your boyfriend. If you don't already have a spa on speed dial, ask friends or coworkers for recommendations. You can also Google spas in your area to read reviews and find out about their amenities. Try to choose a spa that includes a sauna, steam room, and/or hot tub so you can relax prior to and following your massage. You'll melt away any remaining memories of Mr. Ex in no time. (*Mr. Who?*)

Treat Yourself to a Delicious Dinner

Being such a rock star takes a lot of energy. Why not replenish that energy by treating yourself to a delicious dinner? While you may not yet be ready to dine solo in a restaurant, you can still enjoy a fantastic meal in the comfort of your own home (or if you feel like having company, make dinner plans with a girlfriend so the two of you can dine in style!). If you like to cook, stop by the grocery store on your way home, pick up the ingredients for your all-time favorite meal (don't forget a nice bottle of wine and dessert), and whip up that delish dish. If cooking's not your thing, call your fave restaurant, place a takeout order, and enjoy it in the privacy of your own home. It probably feels too soon to sit at the dinner table with relaxing music and candles lit, so don't do it. Instead, find a comfy spot on the couch or in a chair, put on some fun and festive music or a movie that makes you laugh, and spend the evening on a date with yourself. You may just be surprised what great company you keep, not to mention what a catch you really are!

Take a Bubble Bath (but first, get some new bath products)

On your way home from work, stop by one of those bath and beauty stores. Test a new scent or two you've never tried before. If you find something you like, splurge on a new product or products, including a fizzy bath bomb or bubble bath gel to fill your tub with when you get home. Once you're home, draw that bubbly bath, light some candles (preferably a new scent, too), turn on some music, and slip into the sudsy water. So relaxing and incredibly budget-friendly!

BREAKUP RECOVERY TIP

Breakup Recovery Tip: Introduce Yourself to a New Scent

By introducing a new lotion, candle, air freshener, or other scent into your bathroom, you further erase the foul smell of *what's his name*. Love that!

Phone a Friend

You may not be ready to announce the news of the breakup to all of your friends and family, but that doesn't mean you can't dial a friend's digits during your day of denial. Call up a girlfriend you haven't heard from in a while just to catch up (don't even mention the breakup). Or phone a family member and tell him how much you love him. Or, if you need to vent, call a close friend who probably already knows about the breakup and ask if you can spew for a minute or two. While you're at it, recruit her to be part of your Boo-Hoo Crew. Even a diva in denial needs a support system!

WHAT'S A BOO-HOO CREW?

I first introduced Boo-Hoo Crews in *It's a Breakup, Not a Breakdown*. They've been so instrumental to people's breakup recovery that I think they're worth mentioning again. See, every breakup survivor needs a support system and that's where your Boo-Hoo Crew comes in. Part emotional babysitter, part tough-love drill sergeant, your Boo-Hoo Crew should consist of two to three friends who can offer support, guidance, and general ex-boyfriend bashing (as needed).

Who will make up your Boo-Hoo Crew?

Boo-Hoo #1: _____

Boo-Hoo #2: _____

Boo-Hoo #3: _____

Boo-Hoo Crew recruiting tip: Do <u>not</u> choose friends who could possibly turn around and report on your post-breakup progress (and setbacks) to your ex. These are not your friends and should definitely not be part of your Boo-Hoo Crew. Instead, choose friends who have your best interests at heart, are emotionally ready to offer round-the-clock support, and can help you through the pain, agony, and challenges of breakup recovery.

If you don't have people you trust to be part of your Boo-Hoo Crew, go online for support. The message board on my site *www.LisaSteadman.com* features a great support network of people helping each other through their breakups. You can also do an online search for breakup support to find a community that works for you and your needs. Plus, if you'd like to join one of my Boo-Hoo Crew Coaching groups offering weekly telecalls, e-mail support, and ongoing help, visit *www.Lisa Steadman.com/BooHooCrewCoaching* for details.

Spend Some Alone Time with Your New BF with Batteries

Who needs 170+ pounds of loser when you can have a brand new boyfriend with batteries? Before you blush and skip ahead to the next section, hear me out. Just because you're suddenly single doesn't mean you can't still get your rocks off. (Yes, I'm referring to and advocating self-stimulation!) If you don't already have a bf with batteries, you may want to stop by your local adult toy store and pick one up on your way home. Don't be embarrassed. As a diva in denial (and thoroughly modern woman), you have needs. They don't go away just because you're no longer in a relationship. Self-satisfaction is perfectly healthy, normal, and a great source of tension release. So go ahead—get down with your bad self!

Do Something Daring

Did you know that being in a state of denial is the perfect time to try something daring? And no, I don't mean drunk dialing your ex, driving by his house to see if he's home, or cyberstalking him on MySpace (don't even think about it!). I mean do something daring as in try something you'd never done before but may have always secretly wanted to; for example:

1. Go to a karaoke bar, put your name on the list, and belt out a fearless female anthem song like *I Will Survive* by Gloria Gaynor, *'What's Love Got to Do with It?* by Tina Turner, or *Survivor* by Destiny's Child.
2. Sign up to run a marathon (and then create a realistic training schedule you can stick to).
3. Paint your bedroom a bold color.
4. Enroll in a foreign language class (and start researching vacation spots where they speak that language).
5. Become a platinum blonde, fiery redhead, or ballsy brunette, thanks to the help of a colorist.

List a few things you've always secretly wanted to do:

_____

_____

_____

_____

Chances are there's a bold, burning desire lurking inside you somewhere. Only you know for sure what it is. Today, why not be daring enough to admit it out loud and give yourself permission to go for it in the coming weeks (or even today!)?

Chapter *Check-In*

Woo-hoo! You just made it through Day 2 of your twenty-one-day plan to get over your man. Hopefully, you had a little bit of fun. And if you shed some tears, that's okay, too. It's all part of the process. Tomorrow you're going to ditch denial and get back to the business of your breakup. But for now, savor the remaining moments of a day when your ex's name, memory, and whole life don't even exist. While you probably feel some relief, it probably also feels bittersweet. After all, the pain may be gone, but so are the good times you two shared. Whether you know it right now, one day in the not-so-far-off future you're going to look back on all this and realize that you went through the relationship and the breakup for a reason. You'll be stronger, more confident, and even thankful that your ex existed. You'll be grateful that he was such an instrumental part of your life once upon a time, and that he's now gone. That day is probably not today. But take comfort in knowing that day is in your future. It's definitely something to look forward to.

Tonight at bedtime, in addition to reclaiming your independence by sleeping in the middle of the bed, I want you to create a new nighttime ritual. Just as I suggested you create a new morning ritual to further distance your ex's memory, a new nighttime ritual is equally important. Incorporate these new bedtime rituals or add your own!

1. Turn out all the lights, light a candle, and meditate for at least five minutes. Just let your mind go! Or, if you prefer, say a prayer instead.

2. Move your bed to the opposite side of your bedroom, make the bed with new clean sheets, and snuggle in for the night.

3. Introduce a new scent into your bedroom. It can be in the form of a candle you burn before bedtime (just remember to blow it out), an essential oil, or incense.

4. If you don't already keep a journal, start one. Write about all the things you're feeling, both as a result of the breakup, and about life in general.

5. Practice gratitude, starting with "I am grateful for," and mentally list at least five things. Examples may include *I am grateful for my friends, my cat/dog, my job, my family, my freedom, my health.* Simply ask yourself, *What am I grateful for?*

6. _____
   _____

7. _____
   _____

And one last thing. Mark your recovery challenge calendar, depending on how you did today. If you avoided any and all contact with your ex, it's a gold star day! If you let your ex in even a little bit, circle today in red and promise to do better tomorrow. Then climb into bed, pull the covers snuggly-tight all around you, and tell yourself how proud you are of your strength and perseverance. Sleep tight! See you in the morning.

worksheet 1
reflect on your day in denial

Write down what you envision your life would be like right now if your ex had never existed. How would it be better? How would it be worse?

DATE _____

_____

_____

_____

_____

_____

_____

_____

_____

_____

_____

worksheet 1
reflect on your day in denial—continued

_____

_____

_____

_____

_____

_____

_____

_____

_____

_____

_____

_____

_____

_____

_____

_____

_____

_____

worksheet 2
why it's good he's gone

Make a list of all the reasons your life would stink if
you and your ex had stayed together forever. What
compromises did you make or would have had to
make over the long haul? What annoying habits
did he have that drove you crazy? Let 'er rip, Girl!

DATE _____

_____

_____

_____

_____

_____

_____

_____

_____

_____

_____

worksheet 2
why it's good he's gone—continued

_____

_____

_____

_____

_____

_____

_____

_____

_____

_____

_____

_____

_____

_____

_____

_____

_____

DAY 3
delete your EX
from your ONLINE
(and Offline) LIFE

Today, I feel . . .

_____

_____

_____

Breaking up has always been hard to do, but in the new millennium healing and moving on have become even more complicated, thanks to technology. It's just too easy to keep tabs on your ex (without him ever knowing), all from the comfort of your own computer screen (or iPhone). By simply logging on, you can have 24/7 access to your ex's online life via social-networking sites like MySpace, Facebook, and Twitter, not to mention any personal blogs he may have. While it's only natural for you to wonder what he's doing, it's essential to your recovery *not* to waste any of your precious time lurking on his social-networking pages to see what he's up to, who his new top friends are, or if there are any photos or comments from cute girls. It's called cyberstalking and it's a big post-breakup no-no.

Let me say that again. Tracking your ex's online activities is a very bad idea and will ultimately leave you with more questions than answers. Don't do it!

To make moving on a little easier, today's the day you're going to remove your ex from your online and offline life. I know it sounds daunting, but it's absolutely necessary to your recovery. Don't worry—you're not going on this journey alone. I'll take you step-by-step through the process. If at any time you feel overwhelmed, take a break, breathe deeply, and then get back to the task(s) at hand.

 SETBACK ALERT

Right about now, you may be telling yourself that it's far too soon to cut online ties with your ex. Maybe you're under the impression that the relationship isn't really over yet, or maybe you've convinced yourself that, by somehow staying connected to your ex online, you don't actually have to let go and move on.

As your guide on this journey, I'm here to tell you the tough love truth, whether you're ready to hear it or not. By staying connected to your ex online, all you're really doing is sabotaging your

chances of post-breakup success. If you choose to ignore the suggestions offered in this chapter on ex-tricating your ex from your online life, that's your choice. But you're only hurting yourself and making it that much more difficult to move on. Ultimately, it's up to you. I hope that you will choose to put your post-breakup recovery needs ahead of your desire to save face in front of friends or stay connected to your ex. At the very least, I hope you'll read through the chapter to better understand why it really is in your best interest to disentangle yourself from your ex, both online and offline.

The truth is, removing your ex from your online life may not be an easy thing for you to do, but it's absolutely essential to your *happily ever after* future. Even if you just start the process today, that's a step in the right direction. That's all I ask. The more you do, the better. But if baby steps are necessary, then baby steps it is. By all means, if you need moral support, recruit a friend to sit with you at the computer and go step-by-step through the process together.

Perform Your Online Ex-orcism

Depending on how intertwined your online lives were, you may or may not need to take every step in the following ex-orcism. I've tried to be as thorough as possible, so if something doesn't apply to your situation, skip it and move on.

Step 1: Remove Your Ex from Your Friends List on All of Your Social-Networking Sites

The best way to start your online ex-orcism is to sign into all of the social-networking sites you use (MySpace, Facebook, Friendster, Twitter, etc.) and remove your ex from your friends/contacts lists. The good news is that you don't even have to tell him. In fact, don't. It's none of his business, and since these sites don't alert someone when you've removed them, he won't know when (or if) you did it. So go ahead—delete, delete, delete!

List the social-networking sites in which you're still connected to your ex:

_____

_____

_____

_____

Step 2: Update Your Relationship Status on All of Your Social-Networking Sites

While you're signed into your social networks, update your relationship status on each site, too. You're single and ready to mingle! Okay, maybe it's too soon to mingle but you're still single and should celebrate that fact.

Potential Setback: While you're logged in, do *not* seize the opportunity to blog about the breakup or Twitter away about your ex (or check to see if he's blogging or Twittering about you). It's too soon after the breakup and any bitterness will only come back to bite you in the butt. If you feel the need to spew, phone a friend or write in your journal for now.

BREAKUP RECOVERY TIP

 ### Password Protect Yourself

Twenty-first-century couples have been known to share their e-mail and/or social-networking passwords with one another. Do yourself a favor and change all of your passwords today—just in case. That way, your ex can't log into your account(s) to cyberstalk you. When you create your new password, avoid any references to your ex (his name, his dog's name, his birth date, etc.). You don't need to be reminded of him every time you go online.

Step 3: Delete Your Ex's E-mail Address from Your Online Address Book

Next, log into your e-mail account and remove your ex's address from your contacts. I know this may seem harsh, but you don't need it anymore. Plus, this will help you avoid the tragic setback of e-mailing him in a weak moment just to say hi, telling him you miss him, or trying to set up a booty call. Right here and now, do yourself a huge favor and delete his e-mail address. Today. (Seriously!)

Step 4: Remove Your Ex from Your Instant Messaging Friends List

The next order of business is to extricate your ex from your instant messaging contacts list. Sign into whatever instant messenger program you use (Yahoo, MSN, AOL, Trillian, etc.), right-click on your ex's username, select Delete and, if the option allows, choose Delete from Address Book, too. That way, you don't have to obsess every time you see your ex online, wondering what he's up to and/or who he's instant messaging with.

Step 5: What *Not* to Do

After a breakup, especially a bitter breakup, it may be tempting to defame your ex online by blogging about the breakup, filming a post-breakup rant and putting it on YouTube, or spreading vicious rumors about your ex to everyone you know. *Don't do it*. While the initial euphoria of redemption may feel fabulous, the resulting repercussions can be detrimental to your recovery. Your ex may retaliate, your friends may turn on you, and/or you may even sabotage a future relationship because the person you're interested in discovers your online rant and determines that you're around the bend. Trust me, it's just not worth it!

Find a New Online Community

To help fill the void that's been left by removing your ex from your online life, you may want to find a new cyber-support system. I mentioned this briefly in the first chapter, but think it's worth mentioning again. While there are plenty of websites dedicated to healing and moving on after a breakup, ultimately, it's up to you to find the right fit. Of course, you're always welcome to join the message board community on *www.LisaSteadman.com* to share stories, get advice, and find ongoing support. You can also find out about my upcoming breakup coaching groups at *www.LisaSteadman.com/BooHooCrewCoaching.*

Additionally, sites like *www.Been-dumped.com* and *www.FirstWivesWorld.com* also offer excellent articles, advice, and community resources. Sites like *www.first30days.com*, *www.iVillage.com*, and *www.TangoMag.com* also have sections dedicated to healing from a breakup. But because everyone's post-breakup needs are different, your best bet when looking for a cyber-support system is to start with Google, type in your search words (breakup

---

BREAKUP RECOVERY TIP

 ### Avoid the Post-Breakup Drive-By

Oftentimes, we're tempted to keep tabs on our ex by driving by their house, office, places your ex hangs out. Don't do it. If your ex's home or workplace happens to be on your daily route, do yourself a favor and change your route. Take side streets, a left turn instead of a right turn. Even if it takes you an extra five minutes to get where you're going, it's worth it. You're worth it!

---

survival, breaking up, divorce, etc.), and see what speaks to you.

Perform an Offline Ex-orcism

Now that you've removed your ex from your online life, it's time to do the same for your offline life. Depending on how long you were together and how entwined your lives were, this may take more time. For some, it may be as simple as deleting his phone number from your cell phone. For others, it may be more complicated and include moving, returning each other's house keys, contacting insurance agents, banking institutions, and/or changing beneficiary designations on property and other assets. These things obviously take longer than one day to finalize. However, it's incredibly important to do a thorough job of removing your ex from your offline life to ensure that he no longer has access/influence over your personal information, finances, and credit rating.

Here is a list of ways you may need to remove your ex from your offline life:

Delete His Phone Number from Your Cell Phone

This is easy enough to do. While you're at it, be sure to delete his address from your online address book or contacts manager.

Decide Who's Moving Out

Breakups become a whole lot trickier when you cohabitate because one of you now has to find a new place to live. Regardless of how much you hate your ex right now, it's important to be fair about the mov-

ing-out process and expedite it as quickly as possible. The general rule of thumb is whoever lived in the home first gets to keep the place. However, if you moved in together, you'll have to come to a levelheaded agreement about who stays and who goes. Once you do, you owe it to yourselves to make the move as quick and painless as possible. Don't drag it out indefinitely in hopes of wooing your ex back. Instead, treat it like ripping off a Band-Aid. Do it in one fell swoop.

Property owners beware: If you bought property together, the plot thickens. Before either of you moves out, you will need to seek legal counsel to find out what your rights are in the state where you live. This is very important. Don't act irrationally or in haste. You could lose the rights to your property!

Return Each Other's House Keys

If you didn't live together but exchanged house keys, arrange a time to mutually exchange keys and any other property your ex left at your place (and vice versa). It's better to do this exchange in a public setting so you're not tempted to hook up, fight, or both. However, if the idea of seeing your ex makes you want to vomit or hyperventilate, ask a Boo-Hoo Crew member to handle the key/personal belongings swap for you.

Determine How to Split Assets

If you and your ex share bank accounts or other assets, you'll need to come to an agreement about how to divide the money/other assets and then contact the relevant banking/other institution(s) to find out how to legally proceed. Again, it's important to keep a level head about these things and not act out of anger, spite, or bitterness. These are financial decisions. Respect yourself as well as your ex, and be fair throughout the process (no matter how much you really want to punch him in the face!).

Remove Each Other from Miscellaneous Policies

Car insurance, health insurance, retirement plans, credit cards, personal loans, household bills are all potential accounts or policies that you and your ex may share. When you break up, it's essential to remove the other person from each and every one of these items. If you don't, one or more of the following scenarios could come back to haunt you in the future:

o You are turned down for a home or car loan because your ex, still attached to an account you shared while you were together, negatively affected your credit.

o A collection agency comes after you for a debt your ex never paid.

o You become financially responsible (and ultimately financially drained) for a medical emergency your ex encounters weeks, months, years down the road.

o If you die in an accident and haven't changed the beneficiary on your assets (your home, retirement plan, savings account), your ex can possibly claim those assets, leaving a rightful heir with nothing.

As uncomfortable as conversations about money, property, and other assets can be when going through a breakup, you must have these difficult discussions if they apply to your situation. Do your best to broach the subject with fairness and compassion, and insist that your ex does the same. Obviously, the situation becomes stickier if and when one of you uses the unresolved issues as a way to seek revenge, hold on to the other person, or prolong the separation process. If you feel that things are getting out of control, you may need to involve a mediator. Trust your gut about the situation and proceed with the necessary caution. Good luck!

Identify and Distance Yourself from Frenemies

Often when you go through a breakup, you have to distance yourself from more than just your ex. You may discover you've got a few "frenemies." These are friends who pretend to have your best interests at heart but who actually revel in your pain, report on your progress and setbacks to your ex, or in general delight in your current dilemma. Some frenemies are obvious—your ex's best friends, his family, his ex-girlfriend-turned-confidante. However, some are more sinister, playing the role of concerned friend when in actuality they're talking behind your back, cozying up to your ex, sabotaging your progress by talking to you about your ex. Start paying attention to the frenemies in your life. When you find one, run the other way (as fast as you can!).

 ## Chapter *Check-In*

Removing your ex from your online and offline life can be very challenging. I actually thought about moving this step to later in your recovery process, but then I remembered all the messy mistakes I made when going through my Big Breakup. Even though it was before social-networking sites were all the rage, I still committed some cardinal breakup sins like trolling message boards I knew Mr. Ex frequented to see what he was posting, obsessing about who he was talking to every time he logged onto Yahoo Instant Messenger, and because I didn't delete his e-mail address right away, I sent him a few desperate messages when I was freaking out at 2 A.M. That of course led to some regrettable booty calls, followed by hazy regret. And that's why I left removing your ex from your online and offline life on Day 3. As painful as it can be, it's incredibly necessary for your recovery.

Pat yourself on the back for doing such courageous work today. Even if you didn't complete all of the suggested activities, I hope you're well on your way to doing so. And give yourself a gold star on your recovery challenge calendar whether or not you avoided contact with your ex. Today is one of those days where you may have had to be in contact to resolve some unfinished business. As long as your ex isn't in bed with you right now, you definitely deserve a gold star!

Now for your end-of-day activity: Do something incredibly pampering tonight at bedtime. Take another bubble bath. Put on a brand-new pair of cute and comfy PJs. Light a candle and practice your gratitude list for the day, starting with *I am grateful that I had the courage to remove my ex from my online life.* Add another pillow to the bed and snuggle with it all night long if it makes you feel better. Or just let yourself have a good old-fashioned cry. You've earned it. And then, of course, spread out in the middle of the bed, tuck the covers all around you, and enjoy a well-earned night of sleep. Sweet dreams!

worksheet 1
make an ex-orcism list

Make a list of what you still need to do to completely delete your ex from your online and offline life. Do you still need to delete your ex's number from your phone or give him back his golf clubs that have been sitting in your storage unit? Decide what you need to do and check off every item on the list in the coming weeks.

DATE _____

_____

_____

_____

_____

_____

_____

_____

_____

_____

_____

worksheet 2
make a frenemies list

Make a list of people to avoid right now. This list should include anyone who might be detrimental to your breakup recovery. From your parents (if they're not supportive) to your ex's best friend to your ultra-competitive frenemy, keep this list handy. If they call, e-mail, or stop by, screen, delete, or duck!

DATE _____

_____

_____

_____

_____

_____

_____

_____

_____

_____

_____

_____

DAY 4
widow
for a DAY

Today, I feel . . .

_____

_____

_____

Unlike the pity party you threw yourself on Day 1 when you focused all of your efforts on feeling the pain while exorcising your ex from your home and heart, and Day 2 when you denied your ex's actual existence, today you get to channel a different kind of loss. Instead of being a breakup survivor, on Day 4 you're going to transform into a relationship widow. You're even going to hold a funeral, burial, and wake in honor of your deceased relationship—and that's not all! You'll also write a death certificate, eulogy (to perform at the funeral), and last will and testament to determine the breakup beneficiaries. Sound fun? Crazy? A little of both? Good!

As crazy as it sounds, today is an exceptionally important step in your recovery. By being a relationship widow, you allow yourself to properly mourn the death of the life you had with your ex, a life that encompassed many beautiful, amazing, fun experiences. That's the thing about breakups. They're like little deaths. The life you once had no longer exists. While there are plenty of reasons that's a blessing (with more and more reasons revealing themselves as you heal and move on), there are also plenty of reasons that you're hurting. Maybe you didn't see the breakup coming so the shock and surprise feel overwhelming. Or maybe you initiated the breakup, and now feel a sense of disappointment that *what could've been* will never be. Or maybe the breakup was mutual, with both of you realizing that your lives were going in different directions and that it was simply time to move on. Even so, the sorrow and loss you experience is very real. At times, it can feel suffocating. But before you hyperventilate or hide under the covers until the year 2050, now would be a good time to remind yourself that everything you're feeling is perfectly normal. In fact, it's healthy. In other words, let the grieving begin! The following are some suggested activities to help you channel your inner widow today:

Experience the Five Stages of Grief

During your twenty-one-day action plan, you'll most likely experience the five stages of grief. They are:

1. Denial
2. Anger
3. Bargaining
4. Depression
5. Acceptance

As a widow, you may encounter them all in one day. Or, since you already spent Day 2 in denial, you just might decide to skip straight to anger. Go ahead, engage your rage! Kick, scream, curse your ex, and cry until the anger subsides.

Once you've exhausted your anger, give yourself plenty of time to bargain your way through the disbelief surrounding your breakup. Give yourself permission to be needy, clingy, and downright pathetic as you beg (in your head or on paper—*not* to your ex) your loser of an ex-boyfriend to come back to you. Don't worry. You'll grow tired of being such a bargaining mess and snap out of it eventually. When you do, you'll probably fall into a dark depression. Fighting your feelings won't do you any good. Instead, really live in and love the fear, agony, and darkness. Eventually, you'll pick yourself up, dust yourself off, and experience a level of acceptance that ultimately helps you move on. Don't stress if you don't experience all five stages of grief today. You've got seventeen more days to go. (You're doing great!)

Alert Your Boo-Hoo Crew

Being a widow for a day can be a solitary adventure, or you may recruit your Boo-Hoo Crew for support. Only you will know whether you want to include your support system in the funeral, eulogy, and wake. If you do, call, e-mail, or text the funeral details early in the day so your Boo-Hoo Crew has time to put on their most fab little black dresses, pick up necessary supplies (ex-bf voodoo doll), and arrive with tissues (and cocktails) in hand. Once you've alerted your Crew, get back to being a super-stylish widow!

Write a Death Notice

Schedule some time during the day to write your official relationship death notice (see the worksheet at the end of the chapter). Your death notice should include the following:

Name of Deceased
While it's perfectly acceptable to use your ex's actual name, you may want to get a little more creative. Feel free to borrow these suggested names or add your own!

1. My A**hole Ex
2. Mr. Limp Shrimp
3. Cheating Bastard
4. Mayor McSleeze
5. The Cheap Creep

6. _____

7. _____

Where Death Occurred

Next, you'll want to identify the location where your love died. You may choose to be literal or you can have a little fun with it. Borrow from the following suggested death locations or add your own:

1. In my apartment in the middle of *Grey's Anatomy*
2. Somewhere between my dignity and his emotional unavailability
3. In between the sheets he shared with that skanky ho
4. Via text message (the clueless coward!)
5. In a drunken stupor after a night of partying with the guys

6. _____

7. _____

Cause of Death

Just as it's important to identify who died and the location of your relationship's demise, you'll also want to perform an autopsy to determine the cause of death. This can be a little trickier. Right about now, you may have a lot of unanswered questions. Confused about what went wrong, you may be craving closure and clarity. That's why you'll want to spend some quality time today performing an emotional autopsy on your now-deceased relationship. You may not get all of your questions answered, but you may gain some insights that hadn't come to you before. When in doubt, borrow from the following causes of death or add your own:

1. Ongoing emotional neglect
2. An inability to keep his d*#! in his pants
3. Smug overdose
4. Drowned (in his own bs)
5. Lethal rejection

6. _____

7. _____

Once you've written your death certificate, look it over, date it, and make a copy. You'll want to keep one copy for your relationship records and bury one at tonight's funeral.

Write a Eulogy

Next you'll want to write a eulogy to deliver at the funeral (see the worksheet at the end of the chapter). Throughout the day, keep your journal handy to jot down your thoughts as they come to you. The goal is to craft a scathing eulogy of your ex and his participation in your failed relationship, including every hurtful, nasty, and pathetic thing he ever said, did, or was. By getting in touch with all that breakup bitterness (and fully engaging your rage), you're allowing yourself not only to feel and deal with the pain but you're showing the universe (and your ex, the bastard!) that you're going to do more than just survive. You're going to thrive—BIG TIME!

If you're having trouble coming up with eulogy ideas, feel free to borrow from the following list or add your own!

1. (name) was a kind and gentle soul. That is until his overinflated ego got the best of him and he became an absolute nightmare to be around . . .
2. They say breaking up is hard to do, but (name) had no problem dumping me like old, dirty, smelly garbage . . .
3. My mother never liked (name) and now I know why. I won't bore you with the details, except that here are the top ten reasons he was an absolute ass . . .
4. Here lies (name). Good f$%@ing riddance!
5. I've met some jerks in my time, but (name) takes the cake . . .
6. _____
7. _____

The Funeral Procession

To fully prepare for your evening activities, you'll need to run a few errands to gather some supplies. First, stop by a toy store and pick up a male doll. It doesn't have to be an expensive purchase and it doesn't even have to look like your ex. Next, stop by the grocery store or your fave restaurant and get delish dinner fixings for you and your Boo-Hoo Crew. Don't forget the wine or cocktails—this is a celebration!

While you're out, you may want to stock up on more boxes of tissue. And if you're planning a cremation, make sure you have matches and a funeral pyre. Come to think of it, you'll want to have plenty of candles, too, and a fire extinguisher handy.

Once you collect your funeral supplies, head home. Put dinner in the fridge to keep cool or in the oven to warm. Then break open that bottle of wine or mix yourself a strong cocktail, light some candles, and enjoy some much-needed "me" mourning time before your Boo-Hoo Crew arrives. To create even more ambiance, put on some somber music. Or if you're in a celebratory mourning mood, put on something with a good beat so you and your friends can dance your bodacious booties off!

The Funeral

Once your Boo-Hoo Crew arrives, it's time to get down to burial business. First, take your doll out of his box but set the box aside. You'll want to use it as a coffin when the time comes (you can use an old shoe box if you prefer, but remember that your ex doesn't deserve much!). Next, take whatever measures necessary to prep the doll for his proper burial. Since your relationship is already dead, let your grief loose on this symbol of its demise. Want to chop his hair off? Go for it! In the mood to stick pins through his eye sockets? You and your gal pals should take turns. Intent on mutilating his genitals? Good luck there, as the doll probably doesn't have any (kinda like your ex, huh?).

Once you've ~~tortured~~ prepped the doll to your satisfaction, place him in his makeshift coffin. If he complains, remind him that he was never very good about saving for a rainy day and this is all you could afford. That'll shut him up.

Next, fold up the death certificate you created and place it in the box with your ex. Then place the box on the floor or on the funeral pyre (be sure to have that fire extinguisher handy). Toast to his demise, break out the eulogy you wrote earlier in the day, and deliver it in your most dramatic and diva-rrific voice in front of your Boo-Hoo Crew. Really rip your ex to shreds! Talk about the toenail clippings he perpetually left in the tub. Or that he always forgot important dates like birthdays and anniversaries. You can imitate his most ridiculous sex face. And if there are particular passages of the eulogy you want to emphasize, stamp your stiletto-heeled foot on the coffin/box (to the whistles and cheers of your Crew). Or better yet, kick the coffin across the room. In fact, take turns kicking it all over your house! That's considered cardio, you know. The widow's workout: Burn calories while you burn your ex. It's a win-win.

Once you've delivered the eulogy, decide how you'd like to dispose of the body. You can toss it in the garbage, burn it in your trashcan, bury it in the backyard, or take it for a ride out into the country and ditch it. But don't waste too much time with the burial. What comes next is the best part of your day. It's time for the wake. Let the party begin!

The Wake

It's surprising how hungry you can get when trashing your ex, isn't it? Well, now it's time for you and your friends to enjoy that delicious dinner. Set the table with your finest linen, fill every wine or cocktail glass, light some more candles, and toast once again to the recently deceased. Better yet, toast to yourself—the saucy, strong breakup survivor that you are! If you're in the mood, listen to music during dinner. Or if you want to watch a movie, go

ahead. Or if you want absolute silence to reflect on and honor the dead, that's your choice. Do whatever feels right for you.

Movies to Mourn By

Just as you may have parked it on the couch and watched movies during your pity party, today's another day to celebrate your inner couch potato. Only this time, you're in serious mourning mode and will want to choose appropriate movies about lost love, love gone wrong, or long lingering illnesses. Mourn by the following movies or add your own!

1. *An Affair to Remember*
2. *Beaches*
3. *The Bridges of Madison County*
4. *The English Patient*
5. *Ghost*
6. *Legends of the Fall*
7. *Love Story*
8. *Same Time Next Year*
9. *Steel Magnolias*
10. *Titanic*
11. _____
12. _____

After you finish dinner (but before dessert), you've got one more assignment for the evening. And because I believe in saving the best for last, I think you're really going to enjoy it! Just as we inherit valuables when someone close to us passes away and split assets during a divorce, after a breakup we deserve to do the same. So grab a pen and your journal (or use the worksheet included at the end of the chapter), find a comfy spot, and write your relationship's last will and testament. Recruit your Boo-Hoo Crew to help. Together, get creative in what you bequeath to your ex versus what you keep for yourself. Here are some examples, but feel free to brainstorm your own for the worksheet at the end of the chapter.

POSSIBLE THINGS YOU WANT TO KEEP:

o The dog
o The airline miles you jointly accumulated
o Your dignity
o The flat-screen TV you paid for (even though at the time you agreed to go Dutch)
o Your mutual friends (except for his dumb-ass best friend—good riddance!)

o _____

o _____

POSSIBLE THINGS YOU BEQUEATH TO YOUR EX:

o His horrific morning breath
o His beer belly
o His bland cooking
o His inability to take out the trash without being told to
o His bad jokes

o _____

o _____

Once you've reviewed and revised the will to your satisfaction, put it aside and enjoy the rest of your wine or cocktails with dessert. As you savor the rest of the evening with your friends, toy with the idea of sending the will to your ex. Imagine the horrified look on his face when he reads it. Take pleasure in his displeasure. Finally, enjoy the idea that your ex is no longer living and that you're a widow who's almost done with her grieving. If you feel the need to shed more tears, go for it. Or if you're so inclined to dance on your ex's recently dug grave, feel free. There's no right or wrong way to grieve. Just do what feels right for you. Tomorrow's another day and another chance to wake up, break up, and move on.

 Chapter *Check-In*

Whether you decide to mourn privately or with the help of your Boo-Hoo Crew is up to you. The most important thing to remember today is that you are not alone. Many breakup survivors have come before you, and many will follow you. The pain, anger, sadness, and grief you're experiencing are universal. Let yourself feel every emotion, and then release it, knowing that like the many heartbreak survivors who came before you, you too will survive and thrive. You just have to give yourself time. Don't forget to give yourself a gold star or circle on your recovery challenge calendar today, depending on how well you did.

One last thing. You may want to have a Boo-Hoo Crew slumber party tonight. Or you may choose to end the evening on your own. Either way, when it's time for bed climb in, claim the middle, and practice your gratitude for the day, starting with *I am so grateful to have buried the dead. I'm now free to move on to the next stage of my recovery. I am ready!*

worksheet 1
create a breakup death certificate

Create a death certificate for your deceased relationship using this form.

Date _____

Name of deceased:
_____

_____

Time of death: _____

Date of death: _____

Where death occurred: _____

_____

Cause of death: _____

_____

_____

_____

worksheet 2
write a relationship eulogy

Write a scathing eulogy about your ex, including every hurtful, nasty, pathetic thing you know about him. Then crack open a bottle of wine and deliver the eulogy with flair over his corpse!

DATE _____

_____

_____

_____

_____

_____

_____

_____

_____

_____

_____

_____

worksheet 2
write a relationship eulogy—*continued*

_____

_____

_____

_____

_____

_____

_____

_____

_____

_____

_____

_____

_____

_____

_____

_____

_____

_____

_____

_____

worksheet 3
draft a last will and testament

Create a will for your dead relationship. Write
down the things you want to keep as well as the
things you're bequeathing to your ex.

DATE _____

I, _____ being of sound mind and body, bequeath the following
to my ex (a.k.a. Clueless Cad, Fat Bastard, Lying Scumbag):

_____

_____

_____

_____

_____

In addition, I, _____ being of sound mind and body, retain
ownership of the following items of value:

_____

_____

_____

_____

_____

_____

DAY 5
get MAD

Today, I feel . . .

_____

_____

_____

During the course of your breakup recovery, you will most likely experience all five of the stages of grief that I mentioned in the last chapter—denial, anger, bargaining, sadness, acceptance. It's called the post-breakup emotional roller coaster, and it's absolutely essential to your recovery. However, I often hear from coaching clients, on my website, and through my message board that after a breakup, it's all too easy to skip denial, anger, and bargaining, and move directly to depression. Crying becomes the number-one preferred activity for days, weeks, months on end. And while torrents of tears are a perfectly healthy and natural response to heartbreak, I often wonder if they're a substitute for anger. Maybe it's easier to feel sad than to get mad, because getting mad means you have to admit that not only did things *not* go your way, but they went horribly, horribly wrong. Maybe getting mad at your ex feels wrong because you still love him and if you allowed yourself to get mad, you'd have to

acknowledge how much he hurt you. Or maybe it's just too painful to admit that life didn't work out the way you had hoped; instead, it's easier to play the victim and sink into a deep depression. There's just one problem. By doing so, you rob yourself of your rage.

The truth is, engaging your rage can be incredibly empowering. Unlike getting stuck in sadness, getting mad allows you to feel the pain, to *really* tap into the icky, uncomfortable, blood-boiling sensation coursing through your veins following your breakup. Plugged into feelings of injustice, betrayal, and loss, you finally summon the strength to get pissed off. And that's a good thing! See, you can't really let go until you first go off—on your ex *and* on the mess he left behind.

In case you haven't already guessed it, today's your day to get M-A-D. You're going to fully engage your rage. You're going to climb inside that madness and investigate the scene of the crime—that is, your breakup. This will help you understand why you might be so angry right now and what to do about it. But don't worry, I won't leave you angry for too long. We'll do some exercises at the end of the chapter to help ex-orcise your anger. By the time your head hits the pillow tonight, you'll feel lighter, freer, and more at peace about the breakup than you did when you woke up this morning. But before you start your day, take your emotional pulse and jot down how you feel now. Sound good? Let's get started!

The Key to Engaging Your Rage

If getting angry doesn't come easily to you, that's okay. Getting in tune with rage is more challenging for some people than for others. Be patient with yourself and understand that not everybody feels anger in the same way. Some people throw full-blown temper tantrums, kicking, screaming, and spewing. Others experience anger more in the form of sadness, crying over their losses rather than getting angry. And then there are those who would prefer to skip all the drama and, instead, emotionally shut down. Of course, bottling up your emotions is a temporary fix. Eventually, the anger explodes like a volcano and is ejected everywhere. It's not pretty, but it's what happens when you try to stuff your feelings.

Instead of that, why not face your feelings head-on? Start by asking yourself what about your breakup pisses you off the most. If you're not sure, here is a list of common reasons people feel angry after a breakup. See which reason resonates most with you.

Reason 1: You Felt or Feel Powerless about the Breakup

Maybe you had no idea it was even coming. So when your ex dumped you, you were stunned, shocked, and silenced. Blindsided by your breakup, you didn't get to actively participate in the end of your relationship. One day it was just over, and you never got the chance to fight for it or make peace with its demise. This can lead to feelings of powerlessness, not to mention resentment toward your ex for what seems like callous behavior. *How could he?* you may be asking right about now, followed by *Did he ever really love me?* While these questions are common after getting dumped, asking them won't lead to clarity. Truthfully, these kinds of questions only lead to more questions (*Is there someone else? Are they together now?*) and to more rage. Do yourself a favor and stop asking questions. Chances are you'll never get the answers you're looking for (and even if you do, you may not like what you discover).

If you're feeling powerless about your breakup, you may need to ex-orcise your angst the old-fashioned way—by kicking butt. And no, not your ex's butt. Cardio butt! The following are some suggested ways to work out those feelings of post-breakup powerlessness or add your own:

1. Sign up for a self-defense class and karate-chop away your rage.
2. Hire a personal trainer and get in kick-butt shape.
3. Go on a killer hike that makes you huff and puff, but ultimately reveals a spectacular and empowering view (talk about perspective!).

4. Go skydiving (strapped to a super-cute instructor, of course!).

5. Enroll in a yoga class and reconnect to your divine power source.

6. _____

7. _____

Reason 2: You Feel Like a Failure at Love

If you've had your fair share of breakups (and really, who hasn't?), another one may make you feel like a failure at love. *Why does this keep happening to me?* you ask, followed by *What's wrong with me?* Especially if your closest friends and family members are all settled down or married, another breakup may make you question why you can't get things right when everyone around you can.

BREAKUP RECOVERY TIP

R̳ Create a New Mantra

The next time you start comparing your relationship failures to your friends' relationship successes, silently repeat this mantra: "I am not a failure at love. My love life has been karmically eventful and that's okay. In fact, it's fabulous! There's plenty of time for me to get it right."

Why am I such a failure? may be the loop playing inside your head. But before you spiral out of control with this tweaked thinking, think about this: Before their current *happily ever after* relationships, your friends and family members experienced breakups. You may not have known them during this time, but the breakups definitely happened. It just happens to be your turn. Not only that, but your friends in successful relationships are just one successful relationship ahead of you. Just one! You can still catch up. So, instead of beating yourself up, cut yourself some slack and be grateful that you have the opportunity to heal, move on, and eventually find your perfect relationship partner.

Reason 3: You're Angry at Yourself for Putting Up with Your Ex for So Long

Another reason you might be angry is that, in hindsight, you see just how much of his crap you put up with. Maybe he acted like a real jerk sometimes. Maybe he was sloppy, rude, ignorant, inconsiderate, demeaning, or cruel. Even though you didn't like it, you put up with it. Instead of blaming yourself for staying so long, get mad at your ex for being such a jerk/creep/pig/Neanderthal. While you're at it, make a list of all the reasons your ex was, is, and will always be such an idiot. The following list should help you get started. My ex sucks because:

1. His nose was permanently stuck up his boss' ass.
2. He's a total mama's boy.
3. He thought the G-spot was a gay bar (which meant he was never going to visit!).
4. His idea of romance was a dirty text message.
5. He screened my calls when he was with the guys, but took his buddies' calls when he was with me.

6. _____

7. _____

By getting clear about who your ex really is at his core (i.e. not worthy of you), it'll be so much easier to see why it's good he's no longer in the picture. He wasn't the right guy for you. And that's fantastic! Now you're free to find someone who's better suited for you—someone who actually deserves to be with someone as amazing as you. You just have to give yourself time to heal, move on, and eventually attract a perfect partner. Love that!

Reason 4: You Feel Abandoned or Rejected

Breaking up can reveal all kinds of deep-seated fears, including fears of abandonment or rejection. *See, you may be saying, everyone eventually leaves me, including my ex!* I've got news for you. If you believe that everyone eventually leaves you, everyone eventually will. But don't worry—you're not doomed to end up alone. You just need to reframe your current belief system, letting go of any limiting or negative beliefs and instead reframing with more positive ones.

To help release your rage, pay attention to the negative relationship messages you're sending yourself right now. They may include:

1. *Everyone eventually leaves me.*
2. *I'm a failure at love.*
3. *I'm unworthy of love.*
4. *The only kind of love I deserve is painful, challenging, unsatisfying.*
5. *I'm doomed to be alone for the rest of my life.*

6. _____

7. _____

Once you've identified the negative relationship beliefs you hold on to, you're free to reframe them with more positive beliefs, including:

1. *I am worthy of love.*
2. *I am enough just as I am.*
3. *I am blessed with lifelong friends.*
4. *I welcome healthy and happy love into my life.*
5. *My perfect partner loves and appreciates the real me.*

6. _____

7. _____

48

By changing your beliefs about love and relationships from negative to positive, your rage will most likely subside. So go ahead, choose your brand-new happy beliefs. If it's too soon in your recovery to embrace such happy and healthy beliefs, don't worry. We'll revisit this exercise in Week 3. For now, just keep reading.

Another Possible Target of Your Rage

Speaking of rage, I know someone else you might be mad at right about now. It's Y-O-U. The truth is, after a breakup it's far too easy to beat yourself up. Maybe you blame yourself, thinking you could've said or done something differently to avoid the breakup. The nagging questions, self-blame, and the all-too-common phrase *If only I'd* take over your brain like a rapidly spreading virus. Sound familiar? Before you can forgive yourself, you first have to face your anger. Start by making your *If only I'd* list. Borrow from these examples or add your own.

1. If only I'd been more patient.
2. If only I'd given him one more chance.
3. If only I'd said I was sorry.
4. If only I'd stopped being so hard on him.
5. If only I'd been more like her. (If there was another woman involved in the breakup.)
6. If only I'd _____

   _____
7. If only I'd _____

   _____

Making your *If only I'd* list will help you see where you're probably cutting your ex too much slack while unnecessarily beating yourself up. Once you've made your list, review it and then try the following exercise: Remove yourself from the breakup and instead insert one of your closest friends. Now, review the list again. If your friend was the one saying, "If only I'd" how would you respond differently? Would you agree with her, or would you tell her that she had done everything in her power to make the relationship work and it hadn't helped? Chances are, you would give your friend a big hug and tell her that everything is going to be okay. You would also tell her to stop saying "If only I'd" because the truth is, what's done is done. There's no going back. It's time for her to forgive herself and move on.

Can you forgive yourself?

Seriously, right here and now, it's time to forgive yourself. It's time to give yourself that big hug, tell yourself everything is going to be okay, and then say, out loud, "I forgive you." This is an incredibly empowering exercise that I strongly encourage you to try. You may even want to do it in front of a mirror so you can look yourself in the eyes, and say, with compassion, "I forgive you." Believe it or not, you deserve to be forgiven! Don't worry if you don't achieve total self-forgiveness today. By getting started, you'll most likely release your rage and start to feel a sense of calm wash over you.

Chapter *Check-In*

Now that you know why you may be mad (and who you're really mad at) following your breakup, how do you feel? Better? Worse? Just plain pissed off? Whether you know it or not, you're doing great! This is tough stuff. To reward your efforts, engage in one of the following pampering activities before bed tonight:

1. Find a comfy spot, light a candle, breathe deeply, and ask yourself: *How am I feeling?* Really listen to the answers, breathing through the difficult ones, and releasing any negative or painful emotions that come up.

2. Start flipping through magazines and collecting images and words that match your new dream life. Put them in a folder and save them for later. You're going to create a vision board in the coming weeks (more on that later).

3. Fill the tub with bubbles, light some candles, turn on your most relaxing music, and pour a glass of wine. Then slip into the sudsy water and melt away any remaining angst.

4. Put on some girl power music, shake your booty, and take another inventory of your home. Are there any remaining reminders of your ex? If so, collect them and dispose of them as you wish. It's time to fully exorcise your ex once and for all!

5. Do something different in your bedroom. Change the sheets, comforter, pillows, your pajamas, the position of your bed, or the music you listen to on your CD alarm clock. By changing the way your bedroom feels, you're going to further distance the memory of your ex. And that's the absolute best gift you can give yourself right now!

Don't forget to mark your recovery challenge calendar depending on whether you successfully avoided contact with your ex today. I hope it was another gold-star day. If not, don't beat yourself up. Just promise to do better tomorrow. Once you're ready for bed, slip into the sheets, get settled, and give yourself a great big hug. Today was a major step in your recovery. If you still feel any residual anger, take a few deep breaths, and release any angst as you exhale. Do this for as long as you need to feel calmer and more relaxed. Sleep tight!

worksheet 1
engage your rage

Did you discover what you're angry at your ex about? If so, make a list of all the reasons you're raging right now.

DATE _____

Reasons I'm raging at my ex right now:

_____

_____

_____

_____

_____

_____

_____

_____

_____

_____

_____

Now, give yourself permission to unleash your rage on your ex by continuing to list all the reasons your ex sucks. Have fun with this!

DATE _____

The many reasons my ex sucks include:

_____

_____

_____

_____

_____

_____

_____

_____

_____

_____

worksheet 2
make a list of reasons your ex sucks—*continued*

_____

_____

_____

_____

_____

_____

_____

_____

_____

_____

_____

_____

_____

_____

_____

_____

_____

_____

_____

worksheet 3
make your if only i'd *list*

Before you can forgive yourself, you may first have to face your rage. Continue making your *If only I'd* list.

When you're done, review the list and ask yourself for forgiveness. Remember, you don't have to accomplish everything today. This is just a starting point.

DATE _____

If only I'd:

_____

_____

_____

_____

_____

_____

_____

_____

_____

_____

DAY 6
get BITTER, then
get BETTER

Today, I feel . . .

_____

_____

_____

First, I invited you to get mad. Now, I'm encouraging you to get bitter? You bet! See, by channeling these uncomfortable emotions, you're getting in touch with the underlying issues surrounding your breakup. In doing so, you'll break free of your paralyzing post-breakup funk and reconnect to your personal power. If you *really* want to get better, you gotta first get bitter! But first, take your emotional pulse and jot down how you feel.

Embrace Your Bitterness

Instead of denying or fighting your bitterness, today's the day to embrace it. Start by asking yourself: *What am I bitter about?* Go ahead—write the question down in the worksheet at the end of the chapter. Then answer it, making a detailed list. Consider the following or get started on your list now, and continue it when you fill out your worksheet at the end of the day.

1. I'm bitter because he found someone else and I'm all alone.
2. I'm bitter because I'm stuck in this apartment with so many memories while he gets to move on in a new environment.
3. I'm bitter because not only did I lose my partner, but I lost my home, my friends, my dog.
4. I'm bitter because I want to get married and have a baby and instead, I'm single again.
5. I'm bitter because I wasted so much time waiting for him to get his act together, and now that he has, he's gone.
6. I'm bitter because

_____

7. I'm bitter because

_____

55

As painful as it can be to admit the reasons you're bitter, embracing your bitterness is another important step in your recovery. If you find yourself struggling to identify why you're bitter, maybe a better question is this: *What do I hate about my ex right now?* That's probably an easy one to answer. The following are some reasons you might hate your ex or you can add your own:

1. I hate him for not fighting harder for us.
2. I hate him for lying/cheating/betraying me.
3. I hate him because now I'm questioning our entire relationship.
4. I hate him for acting like breaking up was the easiest thing in the world.
5. I hate him because he's moving on without me.
6. I hate him because _____
   _____
   _____
7. I hate him because _____
   _____
   _____

Dig Deeper

To fully embrace your bitterness, next ask yourself the following question: *What did I tolerate in the relationship that was unacceptable?* Chances are, there were certain behaviors, beliefs, and attitudes that you didn't like, but accepted as part of life with your ex. These things were relationship red flags that you saw and disliked, but chose to ignore in order to salvage the relationship. Now that the relationship is over, you're free to be honest about what you

were tolerating. While every relationship requires a certain level of compromise, everyone's tolerance level is different. Take some time to identify what you were tolerating in your last relationship. Consider the following or get started on your list here, and continue it when you fill out your worksheet at the end of the day.

1. He never encouraged me to pursue my dreams and yet I stayed.
2. Even though I put my foot down, he still lied/cheated/belittled me.
3. I put my entire life and goals on hold to take care of him.
4. He refused to meet my needs, but I stayed anyway.
5. His words and actions told me that I was never good enough, and still, I stayed.
6. _____
   _____
7. _____
   _____

Do any of these sound familiar? In reading through them, did you think of others? Start jotting down what it was that you tolerated in your last relationship that made you unhappy and dissatisfied (see the worksheet at the end of the chapter). As you make your list, you'll most likely start to feel the post-breakup bitterness seeping from your subconscious into your conscious mind. It can feel icky and uncomfortable at first. But before you can break free of the bitterness, you have to first feel it. So bring it on!

Digging a little deeper, it's now time to ask yourself: *What was lacking in my relationship?* Here's a sampling of what may have been missing or add your own:

1. The ability to express wants, needs, desires without apology
2. A satisfying and fulfilling sex life
3. Emotional comfort and compatibility
4. Comfortable communication about anything and everything
5. _____
   _____
6. _____
   _____

As you answer these questions, you're getting closer to discovering what's really important to you in a relationship. You're also better able to see why your ex wasn't your perfect partner. This work is so essential to creating a clear vision of your *happily ever after* future. Even though the questions are tough, they're worth the effort. Keep digging!

When you're ready, ask yourself the next question: *How did I sacrifice myself in order to make the relationship work?* Chances are you sacrificed a lot. Take a look at the following sacrifices and see if any of them apply to you or add your own.

1. I felt as though I had to hide or diminish some part of myself to make the relationship work.
2. I stifled emotions (anger, sadness, bitterness) to avoid rocking the boat.
3. I subscribed to my ex's life vision and, in turn, gave up my own.
4. I gave up certain people in my life because my ex didn't like them.
5. _____
   _____
6. _____
   _____

When you take a long hard look at your answers, does it become clear that you weren't able to be your most beautiful and brilliant self with your ex? Instead, you were probably too busy making sacrifices and not getting your needs met. Whether you know it or not, you deserve to have a healthy and happy relationship future. You're taking the necessary steps right this very minute to get there.

 ## SETBACK ALERT

As you ask yourself these questions and engage your bitterness, you may be tempted to call, e-mail, or text your ex and go off on him. Don't do it. The purpose of these exercises is not to lash out at *what's his name*. Instead, it's to deal with the loss, disappointment, and other feelings of grief so you can eventually move on. Remember, you can't avoid these emotions. You have to feel them. So go ahead, Bitter Girl. Let 'er rip!

And finally, ask yourself this question: *What couldn't I say to my ex during the relationship?* See what comes up. The following is a list of things you might not have been able to say. Feel free to add your own.

1. I need more than you're capable of giving.
2. I don't like the way you treat me.
3. I don't like the way you touch me.
4. By staying with you, I'm abandoning me.

5. _____

6. _____

When you write down the things you couldn't say to your ex, does it become abundantly clear why the relationship had to end? Are you able to face the painful (and beautiful) truth that he wasn't good for you? I know, in the midst of your bitterness, you may not be able to see that. But it's the fabulous truth, and I'm here to tell you once again that you deserve real and lasting love in your life. Your chances of having it didn't leave when your ex did. The possibility still exists for you. However, you may first need to face your fears of life without your ex. Lucky for you, that's the next order of business.

Face Your Fear Factor

After a breakup, it's all too easy to think that your ex's life is going to get exponentially better while yours is going to spiral out of control into misery and despair. I've got news for you: Your life is going to rock without your ex! But it's up to you to believe it. Before you can let go of your unfounded fears, you may first need to identify what makes you most fearful about life without your ex. The following is a list of common post-breakup fears. See which ones resonate most with you:

1. I'm afraid of being alone forever.
2. I'm afraid my ex will find someone else before I do.
3. I'm afraid that without my ex, I'm nothing.

58

4. I'm afraid time is running out on my chance for love, marriage, and babies.
5. I'm afraid of looking like a relationship failure in front of my friends.

Take a look at those fears. The ones that resonate most probably feel very real (and very painful). I'm going to let you in on a little secret. The greatest difference between people who merely survive their breakup and those who thrive is fear. Not the presence or absence of fear, but how they *handle* the fear. Fear can keep people stuck—both in relationships *and* during their post-breakup recovery. In fact, if you think about it, you probably know somebody who stayed too long in a relationship or struggled to recover from a breakup because they got stuck in their fear of the unknown. They were so focused on their fear that they never gave themselves a chance to wake up to their amazing future.

If you're stuck in the fear of life without your ex right this very minute, you might be asking yourself the following questions:

Who will I be without him?

How will I survive on my own?

What if I never meet anyone again?

Maybe I should just accept that this is as good as it gets.

What are your personal fears?

_____

_____

_____

_____

_____

The truth is that fear of the great big unknown future can be paralyzing. Some people let fear paralyze them forever! In doing so, they miss out on amazing opportunities including new chances at love, career changes, new homes.

Are you going to let fear of life without your ex permanently paralyze you?

Say it with me, loud and proud. . . . *HELL NO!*

I didn't think so. You're much stronger than that. Besides, the worst has already happened. I'm talking about the breakup. And you survived! Not only that, but you are well on your way to thriving. So instead of being paralyzed by fear, give yourself permission to feel the fear and *still* move on to that bright and beautiful future you deserve. And don't worry if fear continues to plague your recovery. We'll be revisiting how to face your fear, let it go, and move on in future chapters.

Chapter *Check-In*

Before you can release your bitterness and move on to the next chapter, I have one more question for you to answer. This is quite possibly the biggest question you're going to ask yourself during your recovery. Are you ready? Here it is:

What do I deserve now?

Tonight, give yourself permission to be bold about your answers. Even if you don't totally believe it yet, make a list of what you'd like to believe you deserve in your next relationship—or in life in general. In doing so, you engage the law of attraction. Congratulations! This is the next step in your journey toward your very own *happily ever after* future.

In case you need some guidance, the following are some examples of what you deserve now:

1. A heaping dose of self-love and acceptance
2. A blissful existence
3. Truth, respect, loyalty from friends and family
4. A drama-free relationship
5. Real and lasting love

This is an incredibly empowering exercise that will help you see just how amazing you are and what you truly deserve in life and love. Even if you've never experienced happy and healthy love, give yourself permission to dream B-I-G. Now it's time to reinvent what's possible for you. Believe it or not, you deserve the best, and anything and everything *is* possible!

Before you move on to the next chapter, mark your recovery challenge calendar depending on if you avoided contact with your ex or had an unfortunate run-in today. I hope you earned another gold star. But even if it's a red-circle day, don't beat yourself up. You did a lot of great work today. As you get into bed, continue to ask yourself what you deserve moving forward. The key to your bright and beautiful future lies in your ability to believe you deserve the absolute best. As you release your bitterness, start believing and dreaming B-I-G!

worksheet 1
embrace your bitterness

Before you can get better, you first have to get bitter! Answer the following question:

What am I feeling bitter about? If nothing comes to mind, answer this question: *What do I hate my ex for right now?*

DATE _____

_____

_____

_____

_____

_____

_____

_____

_____

_____

_____

_____

_____

worksheet 2
identify your tolerations

Revisit the section on tolerations on page 56 and make a list of what you tolerated in your relationship with your ex. Come up with at least five things. The more, the better!

DATE _____

_____

_____

_____

_____

_____

_____

_____

_____

_____

_____

worksheet 3
continue asking questions

Spend some time continuing to explore at least one of the following questions. As answers come to you, revisit this worksheet.

DATE _____

1. What was lacking in your relationship?

_____

_____

_____

_____

2. What did you have to sacrifice to be in that relationship?

_____

_____

_____

_____

worksheet 3
continue asking questions—continued

3. What was it that you couldn't say to your ex?

_____

_____

_____

_____

_____

_____

4. What are your fears about life without your ex?

_____

_____

_____

_____

_____

_____

5. What do you deserve now in life and love?

_____

_____

_____

_____

_____

_____

DAY 7
get EVEN

Today, I feel . . .

_____

_____

_____

After a breakup, it's all too easy to convince yourself that your ex's life has—or will—become exponentially better without you. Somehow, all of his problems get solved. That big promotion just lands in his lap, his flaws magically disappear, and he's well on his way to *happily ever after* with the most perfect and perky woman. The truth is that's probably not going to happen. But in the midst of your post-breakup angst, you may not be able to see things clearly. That is why now's the perfect time to distract yourself with revenge fantasies!

Let me be clear. Revenge fantasies are perfectly healthy and fun. Revenge realities, on the other hand, can come with jail time, restraining orders, and a tarnished reputation. So rather than take your vendetta into reality, spend the day fantasizing about how you'll get even with your ex to get it out of your system. You'll be surprised at how satisfying revenge plots are, even if they exist only in your mind. Take a look at the following revenge fantasies and feel free to toy with them today.

Revenge Fantasy 1: Plot Your Ex's Death/Demise

Instead of spending any more of your fabulous energy thinking about how your ex's life is going to rock without you, why not refocus those efforts on the many ways he's doomed to end up miserable and alone (or, better yet, dead)? Depending on how you're feeling about your ex right now, you may want his death to be fast, but incredibly painful (that way he disappears from the planet quickly, but still feels tremendous agony), or you might prefer that he suffer a long and lingering life filled with misfortune. Let's start with the idea that he lives an extended yet tragic life, suffering immensely until death finally takes him out of his misery. In that scenario, what terrible, tragic, or otherwise traumatic events befall your ex throughout his rotten life as a result of the breakup?

1. Does he lose his grip on reality, become a chronic bed wetter, and eventually get committed to a mental institution?
2. Does he get fired, evicted, and end up living on the street with his pet rat, Bubba?
3. Does he permanently lose all the hair on his body, including eyebrows, eyelashes, and hair "down there"?
4. Does he miss you so much that he enters the witness protection program just so he can forget about you (Out of sight, out of mind—sure makes your recovery process easier!)?
5. Does he get sent to some remote foreign village on a work reassignment, contract malaria, and slowly and painfully waste away?
6. Does he _____
   _____
   _____
7. Does he _____
   _____
   _____

Better yet, maybe they all happen! Why not? Go ahead—revel in your ex's *unhappily ever after*. Take pleasure in his misfortunes. Or, if you prefer, plot his immediate disappearance from the planet, that is, his incredibly painful death.

1. Does he become the latest victim of a female serial killer who exacts revenge on men who treat women like crap?
2. Does he lose his head at the ex-boyfriend guillotine?
3. Does he find each of his extremities bound and tied to four different cars driven by four members of your Boo-Hoo Crew, who all drive 100 miles an hour in opposite directions at the same time (Feel free to rev your engine!)?
4. Does he become so fixated on his own reflection in the rearview mirror that he misses the Big Rig hurtling straight toward him (Splat!)?
5. Does he go skydiving, only to discover his parachute won't open (Double splat!)?
6. Does he _____
   _____
   _____
7. Does he _____
   _____
   _____

Revenge Fantasy 2: *V* Is for Vendetta

While fantasizing about your ex's horrible fate is incredibly therapeutic, it may not be satisfying enough to stand by and watch his demise. You may want to be actively involved in the pain and anguish he experiences. Although you should never take any of the following fantasies into reality, it's perfectly okay to enjoy getting even (in your head) in any of the following ways:

Ruin Your Ex's Reputation

Revenge fantasy: Your first order of revenge business is to go online and trash your ex's reputation to anyone who will listen. Blog, Twitter, post to message boards, and e-mail everyone, telling them what a jerk, schmuck, scumbag your ex really is. Be sure to copy his boss, his mother, his best friend, and his landlord. Tell them how he lied, cheated, stole, belittled, and betrayed you, how he's horrible in bed, the worst boyfriend ever. Spew until there's nothing left!

In this fantasy, your ex-bashing causes him to lose his job, his apartment, his credit rating, his friends, his family, his dignity, his hair. Eventually, he comes running back to you, begging you to take him back, begging for mercy. At this point, you throw your head back, let out a sexy victorious cackle, and push him to the ground where you then place a ridiculously expensive stiletto heel on his chest, press down ever so slightly, and remind him that you were the best thing he ever had. Naturally he agrees and begs for forgiveness. You walk away, beautiful, confident, strong, leaving him a blubbering, pathetic mess. Of course, your new handsome, successful, amazing boyfriend is waiting nearby in the Lamborghini so the two of you can drive off into the sunset together.

Revenge reality check: While this sounds good in theory, in reality it would not end so happily. Instead, your ex would probably catch you in the act of tarnishing his reputation online, get the police involved, and you could wind up with a restraining order or arrested for harassment. Even worse, he could retaliate, sullying your reputation to anyone and everyone who will listen. The bashing could go on for weeks, months, years, with no end in sight. The result would be that neither one of you moves on. And there's definitely no cute new boyfriend with a sports car! If needed, play this revenge fantasy out in your head but DO NOT bring it into reality.

Trash Your Ex *and* His Stuff

Revenge fantasy: In your post-breakup rage, you key his car, slash his tires, bash in his windshield, set fire to his personal belongings, and throw his computer, flat-screen TV, and Xbox out a two-story window, smashing them to smithereens. Your ex watches helplessly as you destroy each and every possession he's ever owned. He begs for mercy, which you, of course, ignore as you continue your rampage, ruining his belongings.

Next, you focus your rage on the man himself, beating him to a bloody pulp. In the end, there's nothing left but smoldering ash, computer parts, and the bruised and battered remains of *what's his name*. A sense of peace washes over you as you return to your fabulous new life, complete with hot boyfriend, killer apartment, and impressive bank account. You have it all, while your ex has nothing and is an absolute nobody.

Revenge reality check: Like it or not, every action has an equal and opposite reaction. If you were to destroy your ex's property or cause him bodily harm, his reaction would probably be to sue your fabulous, but crazy booty for damages. Do you really want to owe your ex money or have to see him in court? I hope the answer's no. Talk about

it's a
BREAKUP *not a*
BREAKDOWN
WORKBOOK

a waste of your energy! Keep this revenge fantasy where it belongs—in your pretty little head.

Spill Your Ex's Secrets

Chances are, you know a thing or two about your ex that he'd prefer you didn't share with the world. Go ahead and engage in the fantasy that you spill his dirty little secrets to anyone and everyone who might be interested, including his mother, his boss, and the police. Here are just a few examples of spilled secrets your ex would prefer you keep. Feel free to add your own!

1. His little problem with STDs (hey, you'd be doing his new girlfriend a real service!)
2. His fetish porn collection (wouldn't his mother love to know?)
3. His frequent liquid lunches charged to the corporate credit card (and his boss wonders why the bill's always so high)
4. That hit-and-run accident a few months ago (the cops have been trying to solve that one, so be sure to give them his license plate number and address)

5. _____

_____

_____

6. _____

_____

_____

Become *Über* Successful Yourself

It's long been said that success is the absolute best revenge. So, instead of concocting yet another elaborate vendetta against your ex, why not focus on your *happily ever after*? That's a much better use of your time and energy. It's time to start envisioning your successful future, complete with a loving relationship, a fulfilling job, a beautiful home, and financial abundance. I promise you this will be far more satisfying than any revenge fantasy.

Write Your Own *Happily Ever After*

Maybe you thought the two of you would end up together forever. Maybe you're still holding out hope. In your fantasy, you and your ex may still be living *happily ever after*, complete with a beautiful home, a loving family, an adorable dog, maybe even the newly painted white picket fence. I hate to break the bad news, but it's over. Plus, you've been plotting your ex's demise, which means he's headed for oblivion while you're on the road to your dream life. It's time to rewrite that *happily ever after* in your head.

Close your eyes for a minute. Envision your dream life. Is your ex still in the picture? If so, erase or replace him. What does that picture look like now? Are you still in the city he loved, or have you relocated to the country, with plenty of rolling hills and fresh air, or the place you always wanted? Is there a cat instead of a dog or maybe both? Is the house the same, or has it changed? Are there children? Maybe your ex didn't want any, but now you're free to dream about them. Is there a man in the dream life? What qualities does he possess that your ex didn't? Now's the time to pay attention to what was missing in your last relationship that you want to attract in your next. Start making a list of the qualities you're seeking. Engage the law of attraction and let it work for you!

The truth is, you can still have your dream life. You just need to rewrite your *happily ever after* without your ex. He wasn't the star. You are. So go ahead, rewrite your story.

Possible revisions include:

1. **Location:** With your ex out of the picture, where do you dream of living?
2. **Partner:** Who is this new mystery man who is perfect for you? He may be nameless and faceless, but chances are, you know a thing or two about him. What amazing qualities does he possess?
3. **Occupation:** Do you have the same job you have now, or are you doing something completely different? If so, what does that look like?
4. **Children:** Now that your ex is out of the picture, is your vision of family changing? Are there more/fewer children? What do *you* want?
5. **Pets:** Maybe your ex was allergic. Or maybe he only liked dogs while you're really a cat person. You're now free to fantasize about all the loving animals in your dream life!

Take some time to create a clear vision in your mind of your new and improved *happily ever after*. As you do, be sure to add these elements to your vision board file.

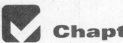 **Chapter *Check-In***

In addition to plotting revenge fantasies, I hope you spent some time today working on your new and improved vision of what *happily ever after* looks like. Keep thinking about this vision in the coming weeks. The truth is, your life doesn't end just because your ex is no longer in the picture. In fact, there are plenty of opportunities for greater happiness and success, as well as deeper levels of joy and authenticity in your life now that the relationship is over. It's just up to you to find them. If you haven't found them yet, you'll just have to take my word for it. There is more joy to be had!

Let me repeat that. After your breakup, there's more joy to experience. Tonight at bedtime, revisit the idea that there is joy for you in the future. Start thinking about the possibilities. Now that you're free from your ex, you can experience more joy in all areas of your life, including:

o More joy in your heart
o More joy in your friendships
o More joy in your career
o More joy in your love life

Go ahead, start dreaming. What areas of your life do you want more joy in?

As with every day, be sure to mark your recovery challenge calendar depending on how well you did avoiding your ex today. Let's hope it was another gold-star day. Keep up the great work! And congratulations! You just made it through Week 1 of your twenty-one-day plan to get over your man. Tomorrow begins Week 2. Woo-hoo!

worksheet 1
plan your ex's demise

Write about your ex's personal demise, plotting each and every horrible thing that happens to him as a result of losing you (*including* getting fired, losing his apartment, losing his hair, losing his mind).

DATE _____

_____

_____

_____

_____

_____

_____

_____

_____

_____

_____

_____

worksheet 2
spill your ex's secrets

Write an anonymous note to his best friend, his boss, the local police department—whoever would be most interested in his secrets. Edit the note. Wait twenty-four hours, and then destroy it. That way, you're not tempted to send it. After all, the fun is in the writing!

DATE _____

_____

_____

_____

_____

_____

_____

_____

_____

_____

_____

worksheet 3
write your own happy ending

Now that you're free, write your own happy ending. Make it as sensational, sexy, and sassy as possible. Will you inherit millions? Meet Prince Charming by next week? Become super successful? You are your fabulous future—you decide!

DATE _____

_____

_____

_____

_____

_____

_____

_____

_____

_____

_____

_____

_____

_____

_____

_____

_____

_____

_____

_____

_____

_____

_____

_____

_____

_____

_____

_____

_____

_____

_____

DAY 8
ANNOUNCE
your breakup

Today, I feel . . .

_____

_____

_____

Welcome to Week 2. The fact that you're still here tells me how strong you really are, and how committed you are to your own recovery. Congratulations! You should be very proud of yourself. How are you feeling today? Jot down any emotions that come to mind as you think about the fact that you've made it this far. Whereas Week 1 was all about simply surviving your breakup (and creating that much-needed distance from your ex), in Week 2 you're going to take your personal power back. You're also going to create a clearer vision of your future. By empowering yourself to heal and move toward that brighter future, you take the focus off your ex and put it where it needs to be—on Y-O-U. In the process, you may even start feeling excited about your life again. That's what Week 2 is all about. Together, we're going to create a vision of your future that is so beautiful and brilliant that, truthfully, your ex wouldn't be able to handle it. And to kick-start your week into high gear, it's time to announce your breakup to the world.

Break the News

Announcing your breakup may not sound like fun, but it can be if and when you approach the announcement with a sense of humor, an ability to laugh through the pain, and just the right amount of ex-bashing. Your big announcement can be as simple as sending a mass e-mail to friends and family, creating a cute and clever e-card, or going all out and mailing official breakup announcement cards to everyone you know. Of course, it's got to reflect your own personal style, so it's really up to you. See which of the following scenarios best matches your style.

Send Your Friends a Breakup Announcement

With your Boo-Hoo Crew already on speed dial, it's time to break the breakup news to everyone else. The easiest way is to send a mass e-mail to the important people in your life. Possible subject lines include the following or make up your own!

1. I just lost 170+ pounds (of loser)!
2. Ding dong, the jerk is gone!
3. Turns out, breaking up isn't so hard to do.
4. I'm suddenly single, let's mingle!
5. Breakup survivor seeks hugs and well wishes.
6. _____
   _____
7. _____
   _____

Now, you may want to dish all the dirty details in your e-mail or simply let everyone know that the breakup happened and, to show their support, your friends should never mention your ex's name to you again. If you had to move as a result of the breakup, be sure to include your new contact information in your announcement. Or, if you're in transition right now (sleeping on a friend's couch, in a temporary living situation, etc.), let your friends know how to reach you and let them know that you'll send more details when you're settled in your new home.

Want to dress up your breakup announcement? Say it with a free e-card! There are plenty of sites that offer free and funny breakup e-cards including *www.Cyranet.com*, *www.GreetingCards.com*, and *www.SomeEcards.com*. Sample messages include "I'll be publicly sobbing for the next few weeks" and "Let's stay friends behind my ex's back." You can also get creative and customize your e-card.

Suggested text for your breakup announcements include:

1. Roses are red, violets are blue. We broke up, how are you?
2. I know you never liked name. Now you can tell me why!
3. I just got dumped. What's new with you?
4. Of all the things I lost during my recent breakup, I miss my sanity / my cat / my dignity the most.
5. I just checked into the Heartbreak Hotel. It's not so bad.

Brainstorm your own ideas here and take them further in Worksheet 1.

6. _____
   _____
7. _____
   _____

Want to take your breakup announcement a step further? You can purchase breakup announcement cards to personalize and mail to friends. Especially if you were in a long-term relationship and you lived together, this may be the route you want to take. It lets you announce the breakup in a more personalized way, alerts everyone of your new contact information if you've moved, and gives your friends and family the opportunity to react and respond to the news in their own time. This is something that's easy to forget when going through a breakup: Other people are affected by the split. And while your Boo-Hoo Crew should put your recovery needs before anything else, you may need to give your other friends and family time to process and grieve before they can help you do the same. I know it sounds crazy, but it's true. Breaking up is hard on more than just you and your ex.

If you're in the market for breakup announcement cards, visit my online shop *www.CafePress .com/breakupshop*. Sample breakup announcements include: *Recently Recycled, Single and ready to mingle!* and *I needed more closet space.* You can also purchase breakup announcement cards on sites like *www.TheDivorceCards.com, www.Greeting CardUniverse.com*, and *www.LolaSays.com*.

Then again, not everyone wants to announce their breakup in an e-mail or a card. If this method of sending a breakup announcement seems impersonal, call in sick to work, open your contacts list, and call each and every friend you know to give them the dishy details over the phone. Of course, this can be incredibly time-consuming but if you're a girl who likes to gab, go for it!

BREAKUP RECOVERY TIP

R⬝ **Don't Buy into Guilt Trips**

Feeling guilty about how other people are dealing with your breakup? Don't worry your pretty little head about anyone else right now. This is your time to heal and move on. Focus on your own recovery process. If and when guilt creeps in, tell it to go away. You're busy becoming a breakup rock star!

Create a Single-Gal Gift Registry

One of my very favorite episodes of *Sex & the City* was titled "A Woman's Right to Shoes." In it, perpetual single gal Carrie Bradshaw discovers that while there are plenty of opportunities to celebrate her married-with-children friends' choices (bridal showers, wedding gifts, baby showers, etc.), there are virtually no opportunities to celebrate the single woman. No single-gal parade, no greeting cards saying *Congratulations on not marrying the wrong guy!* and no gift registry for breakup survival.

That was then; this is now. Enter The Well-Heeled Society, the first online gift registry for single women. Founder Felicia Coley contacted me during my last book tour to tell me about her genius idea. Here's what Felicia says about The Well-Heeled Society:

"If babies, engagements and weddings are not on your To Do List, don't think for one second you have nothing worthy to celebrate. Overcoming that diagnosis, finally publishing your book, or landing your dream job was nothing short of a labor of love. And since prosperity is merely the universe funding your purpose, here is where single women come to announce and celebrate their elite, prosperous and definitive lives with gift registries."

Love that! Check out *www.WellHeeledSociety .com* for yourself. You can sign up for free, create your very own *suddenly single* gift registry, and then send it to friends along with your breakup announcement. Additionally, you can create a wish list on any number of shopping sites and send it to your friends to announce your breakup. Be sure to include any items you lost during the breakup (toaster, bath towels, DVD player, etc.), as well as anything that strikes your fancy and will help celebrate the new you who is emerging (that *to die for* pair of red heels, wineglasses, a new designer handbag, etc.).

Splurge on a Symbol of Your Single Status

Instead of downplaying your newly single status, why not celebrate it? In fact, you can now announce your single status (and potentially improve your dating life) by wearing any or all of the following items:

1. The world's first diamond ring for single gals from *www.DivineDiamonds.com*. Worn on the pinky, the *Ah Ring* allows single women to show the world they're available (*A*) and happy (*h*). Love that!
2. A fun and flirty T-shirt courtesy of *www.SingleTease.com*. Sample tee slogans include *boy scouting (are you prepared?), just ask me (out), single, support your local library (check me out), say hello, looking for good pick-up lines*. What better way to get the conversation started?!
3. The world's first unisex single ring, available online at *www.singelringen.com*. This sleek turquoise ring can be worn on any finger and helps let the world know you're single and happy. Plenty of celebs have been spotted wearing the single ring, so why not sport one yourself (and keep your eye out for hotties with their very own single ring)?

Announce Your Breakup Online

The next order of business in reclaiming your fab single status is to announce your breakup online. If you haven't already, start by updating your single status on your social-networking sites. Next, it's time to blog/Twitter about the breakup. Keep in mind that anything you say can and will be used against you later. It's in your best interest to have a sense of humor about the breakup, to be fair about how things went down, and to protect the guilty, avoid using your ex's real name. If you need help getting started, the following are suggested blog/Twitter openers:

1. I said *I love you*, he said *It's over.*
2. Getting dumped like yesterday's trash really stinks.
3. I kind of always knew I'd end up his ex-girlfriend.
4. A funny thing happened on the way to *happily ever after.*
5. Another ex-boyfriend bites the dust.

Jot down your own ideas here and take them further when you fill out your worksheet at the end of the day:

_____

_____

_____

Or, if you'd prefer to dish about the breakup in a more anonymous fashion, visit one of the many online message boards dedicated to breakup survival. There's an awesomely supportive message board community at *www.LisaSteadman.com*. You can also Google "breakup message boards" to find other online communities. Here's a tip: To ensure anonymity, don't use your real name as your username when signing up on any message board. And don't use your ex's real name; that's a dead giveaway to your identity. Plus, it's just plain tacky to name names, even if your ex is a dirt bag /slimeball /scum of the earth.

 SETBACK ALERT

There may be people in your life who don't support your breakup recovery. You may anticipate who they are (your predictably overly critical friend), and simply avoid sending them a breakup announcement. Or, you may be blindsided by a breakup critic you never expected. Be prepared for these unsuspecting recovery saboteurs. When you encounter them, sidestep their negativity, put them on your list of people to avoid right now, and move on. If they throw you into a momentary emotional tailspin, speed-dial your Boo-Hoo Crew for an impromptu pep talk. Then get back to the business at hand—your fabulous breakup recovery.

 ## Chapter *Check-In*

Because everyone's breakup recovery is unique, your approach to announcing your breakup should be, too. After all, telling the world at large that your relationship recently ended may not be the easiest thing to do. The guidelines in this chapter are simply suggestions aimed at making the process a little bit easier and more fun. Ultimately, it's important to do what feels right for you. If that's shouting your suddenly single status from the mountaintops or keeping the news to yourself for now, do whatever feels right. If and when any activity makes you uncomfortable, stop, take a deep breath, and ask your Boo-Hoo Crew for support. That's what they're there for.

Now, it's time for your nightly assignment. After marking your recovery challenge calendar with a gold star or a red circle (depending on how you well you avoided contact with your ex), get out your journal and spend some time writing about the lessons you may be learning during your breakup recovery. Maybe you now realize he wasn't right for you. Or maybe it's becoming clear that you have some stuff to work through before getting into another relationship. Regardless, record your lessons as they come to you. And then give thanks that yet another day has passed and you're still here, not just surviving but thriving!

worksheet 1
announce your breakup

If you haven't already, now's the time to announce your breakup to friends and family. First, mix yourself a strong cocktail, channel your inner Jackie Collins, and then write a diva-rrific announcement, telling everyone how absolutely fabulous you feel now that *what's his name* is history. Revise and edit it until you are satisfied. Then send. Feel free to jot down your ideas here.

DATE _____

_____

_____

_____

_____

_____

_____

_____

_____

_____

_____

_____

worksheet 2
create your online gift registry

Make a list of any and all personal belongings you lost in the breakup (coffeemaker, CD player, tool-kit, etc.), as well as items you think you deserve for surviving the breakup (that red dress, those suede boots, new bedding, etc.). Then create a gift registry / wish list and e-mail it to friends and family. This is one pity party that deserves presents!

DATE _____

_____
_____
_____
_____
_____
_____
_____
_____
_____
_____
_____
_____

worksheet 3
dish all the dirty details

Write about how you *really* feel—the pain, anguish, betrayal—then go online and share it on a message board or blog where other breakup survivors can read it and commiserate.

DATE _____

_____

_____

_____

_____

_____

_____

_____

_____

_____

_____

_____

worksheet 3
dish all the dirty details—continued

_____

_____

_____

_____

_____

_____

_____

_____

_____

_____

_____

_____

_____

_____

_____

_____

_____

DAY 9
disappear
for a day

Today, I feel . . .

_____

_____

_____

Let's review: In the last four days, you engaged your rage, embraced and released your bitterness, plotted revenge fantasies, and then announced your breakup to the world. Whether you know it or not, that's a lot of heavy-duty post-breakup recovery work. If you're feeling vulnerable right now, that's to be expected. Write down your feelings here. As a reward for your bravery and resilience, give yourself permission to disappear for a day. By turning off your cell phone, avoiding your e-mail, and disconnecting from your social network, you give yourself a chance to peacefully process all the hard work you've been doing without outside interference from opinionated frenemies, judgmental coworkers, and disappointed friends and family members. By spending the day with yourself, you celebrate the work you've done so far, and look forward to the healing ahead. If you can't completely disconnect today because of work or other commitments, that's okay. Make an effort to duck out of the office for a leisurely lunch, only respond to the calls and emails you absolutely have to, and spend the evening away from your phone, e-mail, and other typical social trappings. Today is all about you!

The Benefits of Disappearing for a Day

Staging a disappearing act has numerous benefits, including:

1. You further distance yourself from your ex (both geographically and emotionally).
2. You give yourself permission to envision a bright future without your ex.
3. You escape any external judgment following your breakup announcement on Day 8.
4. You get to heal your heart in an environment that doesn't remind you of your ex.

Now that you know the benefits, you're ready to get lost for the day. For emergency purposes, have your cell phone on you—just make sure it's turned off. Also, if you think disappearing for a day will cause Boo-Hoo Crew to file a missing persons report, alert them ahead of time so they don't worry about you. If they ask to come along, just say no. This is your day to disappear. So slip into some sassy shoes (a girl's gotta feel fabulous, after all!), pack yourself some snacks, water, and activity-appropriate accessories, and hit the road.

Suggested Disappearing Acts

Not sure what to do on your day away? The ideal disappearing act will reintroduce you to activities you once enjoyed (that you may have given up during your last relationship), help reconnect you to your spirituality, and provide some much needed R and R. Plus, spending the day alone will (I hope) reacquaint you with your own innate fabulousness (it didn't go out the window with your ex) and help you start envisioning your bright future. Here are some suggested disappearing acts you may want to consider.

Get Back to Nature

Mother Nature knows a thing or two about how to heal a broken heart. So do yourself a favor and spend some time in nature today. You might be surprised at how peaceful you'll feel as a result. Suggested back-to-nature activities include:

○ **Go on a strenuous hike / nature walk.**
Endorphin rushes are always good following a breakup, and when they're released in the outdoors, it's like they double in potency! Between challenging your body and opening your mind, you'll connect to a sense of inner peace that may have been lacking since the breakup happened. You may even get inspired and start envisioning a *happily ever after* without your ex. Love that!

○ **Spend the day near water.**
If you live near the beach, go to the beach. If there's a nearby lake, spend some time there today. If you can find a waterfall, even better! If there's not a large body of water within driving distance, find a swimming pool. Or take a long relaxing shower or bath. Just spend some quality time near a body of water today. Why? Water has incredible healing properties. It soothes the soul, which is exactly what you need right now. If nothing else, buy yourself one of those miniature fountains at Bed, Bath, & Beyond and put it in your bedroom, home office, or living room. The sound of running water is almost as calming as spending time near a body of water.

○ **Hang out at a park.**
When was the last time your feet touched grass? Chances are it's been a while—probably too long. Today would be a good day to go to a park, slip off your shoes, and let the grass tickle the soles of your feet. This is a great way to reconnect to childhood and, more important, to your inner child. During a breakup, your inner child feels pretty sad. The breakup makes her feel especially vulnerable and isolated because she doesn't have the grown-up wisdom to understand what's happening. Today's the day to give your inner

child the TLC she needs. Take her to the park, walk barefoot through the grass, swing on the swings—nurture her. She deserves it! (And if there happens to be snow on the ground, make a snow-woman with your inner child. Better yet, make snow angels!)

What back-to-nature activities will you do?

_____

_____

_____

Take Off on an Impromptu Road Trip

You know the Zen philosophy: *It's not the destination but the journey that's important*? Well, if you live in a small town (or at least close to your ex), one of the best things you can do for your healing heart is to get the heck out of Dodge for a day. It really doesn't matter where you go, just get in the car and drive. You could stop at a nearby outlet mall, a museum, or cultural landmark, have a picnic, or just get lost in your thoughts for a day.

Reconnect to Your Spiritual Self

If religion and/or spirituality play an important role in your life, today's a good day to reconnect to that part of yourself. Make an appointment with your priest, rabbi, or other spiritual guide. Seek out that person's wisdom and/or guidance. Or if you enjoy yoga, put on some comfy clothes, grab your yoga mat, and get your butt to a class. Today's also a great day to meditate. Go deep into your heart and ask what it needs to heal and move on. Honor whatever it tells you.

Participate in a Movie Marathon

Disappearing for a day can be as simple as heading to your local multiplex and watching movie after movie. Go online first to find out what's playing and then figure out what order you'll watch the movies in, depending on their start and run times. Next, head to the multiplex, buy your tickets, load up on snacks, and enjoy surfing from movie to movie. Even though a comedy should definitely be on your viewing list, feel free to check out a tearjerker, too. Give yourself permission to laugh, cry, and feel any and every emotion that comes up today. Remember, the only way to heal and move on from your breakup is to go through those messy emotions, feel them, and release them.

Spend the Day at a Spa

In the last few years, I've heard from so many people who tell me that after a breakup, they started suffering from migraines, insomnia, chronic pain. You don't want that to happen to you. Instead of letting the pain of your breakup become something you manifest physically, give yourself permission to pamper your body during your twenty-one-day plan to get over your man. By treating yourself to a massage, facial, manicure and pedicure, you de-stress your body *and* nurture your healing heart. It's a win-win!

If you can't afford to spend a day at the spa, enjoy a spa day at home. Draw a bubble bath, recline in your tub with soothing, cooling cucumber slices or warm tea bags over your eyes, and let all your cares slip away. Later, give yourself a manicure, a pedicure, and a facial. You don't have to break the bank to break free of post-breakup body tension. But you do deserve to get pampered!

Revisit a Favorite Pastime

During your last relationship, you probably gave up an activity, hobby, or pastime so you could spend more time with your ex. Maybe it was Pilates on Saturday mornings, Sunday brunch with the girls, or that painting, cooking, or language class you stopped taking because it cut into time with *what's his name*. Today's the day to make a list of those activities you once loved, but no longer participate in. You can even add things to the list that you'd like to try but never did because of him.

Every day moving forward, revisit the list. Promise yourself that you'll pursue any activity or interest that gets your heart racing. In fact, if there's an activity you can engage in today, go for it. If not, make plans to check items off your list in the coming weeks and months. Now's the time to reconnect to all those awesome activities your ex got in the way of. You'll get back in touch with the amazing individual you were long before you met your ex, proving that your fabulousness didn't disappear along with the breakup.

Keep Today Your Day

Don't be surprised if during your disappearing act, your ex tries to reconnect. Ex-boyfriends have a ~~funny~~ scary way of knowing when you're moving on with your life, especially when you're doing something just for you. To help prepare for a close encounter of the ex kind—today or moving forward—the following possible scenarios involve a run-in with your ex, followed by appropriate responses you may want to employ.

If Your Ex Calls . . .

1. Screen the call and then reward your efforts with chocolate.
2. Forward his call to your Boo-Hoo Crew and let them reprimand/scold/torture your ex.
3. Change your phone number.

If Your Ex E-mails/Texts . . .

1. Delete, delete, delete!
2. Mark as spam and block his e-mail address/phone number.
3. Send him the following e-mail reply: *Due to recent events, NAME is longer accepting e-mail from you. Any future e-mail will be forwarded to the Breakup Survivor Squad and may result in a hefty fine, painful penalty, and/or deadly computer virus. Consider yourself warned.* Or, if he texts, send him the following reply: *Leave me alone. Now!*

If Your Ex Stops By . . .

1. Slam the door in his face.
2. Ask him which he prefers—mace in the face or a kick in the crotch. He'll get the picture.
3. Serve him with ex-boyfriend boundary papers, explaining that the 200 yards around you are off-limits at all times from now on.

If Your Ex Enlists His Friends to Call, E-mail/Text, Stop By . . .

1. Hang up repeatedly until they stop calling.
2. Delete, delete, delete!
3. Ask them which *they* prefer—mace in the face or a kick in the crotch. They'll get it.

Chapter *Check-In*

Getting away for a day has numerous benefits. You get to escape your breakup reality, reconnect to who you are without your ex, and revisit old pastimes that made you happy (and can make you happy again). I hope during your day away you rediscovered the pleasure of your own company. Whether you know it or not, your ex didn't make you amazing. You are what makes you amazing! The sooner you realize and celebrate that, the better. To help remind you of this, tonight at bedtime I want you to make a list of the many ways that you are fabulous. Your list can include silly things like *I'm fabulous because I snort when I laugh* or serious things like *I'm fabulous because I volunteer my time*. This list is just for you. So go ahead, write down at least five to ten reasons why you're fabulous. Then settle in to bed with a smile, knowing that you have a very bright future ahead of you.

And don't forget to mark your recovery challenge calendar depending on how you did today. Here's hoping it was another gold-star day. Even if you successfully navigated an ex encounter today, give yourself a gold star. You rock!

it's a
BREAKUP *not a*
BREAKDOWN
WORKBOOK

revisit old/create new goals and hobbies

Make a list of things you used to do or wanted to do but never did because of your ex. Then make a plan to check each item off the list within the year.

DATE _____

_____

_____

_____

_____

_____

_____

_____

_____

_____

_____

worksheet 2
make your fabulous factor list

Give yourself permission to brag about all the reasons you're fabulous!

DATE _____

I'm fabulous because . . .

_____

_____

_____

_____

_____

_____

_____

_____

_____

_____

_____

_____

make your fabulous factor list—continued

I'm fabulous because . . .

_____

_____

_____

_____

_____

_____

_____

_____

_____

_____

_____

_____

_____

_____

_____

_____

_____

_____

DAY 10

RECLAIM your space

Today, I feel . . .

_____

_____

_____

Now that you're almost halfway through your recovery program, it's time to reclaim your space, starting with removing any remaining memories of your ex from your home. Even if you think you've already performed a thorough ex-orcism, there may still be some remaining memories to dispose of today. Once you've ex-orcised any ex-boyfriend residue, you're going to cleanse your space, and start filling your home with visual symbols of the exciting and amazing future that awaits you. It may surprise you how much fun today's activities are and how much freer they'll make you feel. That's a good thing! By releasing any remaining ex-boyfriend burdens and celebrating fabulous Y-O-U throughout your home, you create that bright future right now. Let's get started!

The Case for Reclaiming Your Space

Ultimately, it doesn't matter if you lived together, spent time in each other's homes, or never set foot through each other's front doors (in the case of a long-distance relationship). The importance of reclaiming your space remains essential to your recovery. Here's why:

If You Lived Together and Are Staying Put

If you and your ex lived together and he's the one who moved out after the breakup, reclaiming your space is absolutely essential to your recovery. After all, much of your experience in your home probably revolved around time spent together—waking up, eating meals, sharing space, sleeping. Right about now, your entire house may remind you of him. If that's the case, you don't need to pack up and move—but you do need to take back your space!

If You Lived Together, but You Moved Out

As expensive and inconvenient as moving out after the breakup can be, if you're now in a new space, it's actually a little easier for you to heal and move on. Why? Because you're not surrounded by constant memories of your ex: *This is where we had morning coffee together. This is where we snuggled on the couch and watched movies together on Friday nights. This is where we had our last fight.* By recovering from your breakup in a new place that is free of relationship ghosts, you're better able to reclaim your new space and envision your bright future.

If You Spent Time in Each Other's Homes

Even if you never shacked up, chances are you and your ex spent plenty of time behind closed doors. Sleepover dates, romantic dinners at *your* dining room table on *your* plates. There may have even been future plans to cohabitate. And, while neither of you had the hassle or expense of moving following the breakup (thank God!), there are probably many memories lingering in your home that now need a gentle shove out the front door. That's exactly what we're going to do today.

If You Rarely Spent Time in Each Other's Homes

Your ex didn't have to set a physical foot inside your home to leave a lasting impression. Whether you had roommates and it was too crowded, lived hundreds of miles apart, or didn't spend much time in each other's homes for some other reason, the memory of your ex can still be potent and painful. That chair you always sat in while talking to him on the phone, the photo collage of you two in happier times, the desk where you sat and instant-messaged, texted, or talked via web cam. That's why it's absolutely essential for you to reclaim your space today, too.

The ABCs of Reclaiming Your Single Space

Now that you know why it's important to reclaim your space, it's time to get started. If you don't accomplish all of the tasks mentioned in this next section today, be sure to revisit this chapter at a later date. Remember, your recovery is counting on you to have a healthy space to move on in. The more energy and effort you put into reclaiming your space, the easier it will be for you to heal and get on with your fab future.

Perform a Final Ex-Boyfriend Ex-orcism

In order to leap into your future, you have to first let go of the past. And that starts with letting go of any reminders of *what's his name* throughout your home. By now, you've removed most of the physical evidence of your ex, but there may be remnants that need deleting as well, including:

o Saved messages on your answering machine/ voicemail
o His favorite programs on your TiVo
o That picture of the two of you on your computer screen saver or wallpaper
o The empty drawer or closet space you always made available for his stuff (Fill it, Girl!)

○ Any remaining physical evidence (i.e., photos, clothes, personal belongings)

○ _____

_____

○ _____

_____

○ _____

_____

🔊 SETBACK ALERT

As you perform your final ex-orcism, resistance may start seeping into your system. Don't worry. That's perfectly natural. However, you've come too far and done too much amazing work to hold on to your ex. Right here and now, give yourself permission to be thorough in your ex-orcism. Get rid of everything! If you need help, recruit that Boo-Hoo Crew. That's what they're there for!

Cleanse Your Space

Once his memory is good and gone, it's time to cleanse your space. While I'm not an expert on the subject of *smudging*, I do believe in the healing benefits and have performed the following ritual when going through my many breakups:

○ Purchase a bundle of sage at a new age shop or health food store.
○ Light the smudge (sage) stick using a match or candle. Blow on or wave the flame with your hand to put out the fire.

○ Allow the smudge stick to smolder, letting the smoke circle in the air. Fan the swirls of smoke around your home, body, or personal objects.

In case this feels a little *woo-woo* for you, here's what *www.About.com* says about smudging: "The ritual of smudging can be defined as 'spiritual house cleaning.' In theory, the smoke attaches itself to negative energy and as the smoke clears it takes the negative energy with it, releasing it into another space where it will be regenerated into positive energy."

Reclaim Your Most Sacred Space

Once you've removed any remaining reminders of your ex and cleansed your space, it's time to reclaim your most sacred space—the bedroom. Now, you may have already moved your bed, gotten new sheets, bedding, and pillows, and invested in new pajamas or a new air freshener or candle. Congratulations! If you haven't, what are you waiting for? Change your linens, PJs, and pillows ASAP.

Next, ask yourself what else you can do to reclaim your bedroom. Here are just a few ways you might want to take back your most sacred space today:

1. Paint the walls a vibrant new color that makes you smile.
2. Buy and hang a new piece of art that symbolizes your recovery, rebirth, and beautiful future.
3. Fill any empty spaces left by your ex with fun and fab items, imagery, whatever.

4. Get a throw rug and put it next to your bed so that when you get up in the morning, your feet have a different sensory experience.
5. Find a visual symbol of your recovery and place it in your bedroom (more on that in a minute).

How will you reclaim your space? Get started on your list here, and continue it when you fill out your worksheet at the end of the day:

6. _____

_____

7. _____

_____

Reclaim the Rest of Your Space

While your bedroom is the first order of business when reclaiming your space, the rest of your home deserves some TLC, too. Take an inventory of each room in your home and see if you can do something simple to change the energy, look, or feel of each room. Repossessing your space can be done on any budget so don't skip this step if you're temporarily broke after the breakup. Simply move the furniture; change the noise/music/sound you wake up to in the morning, or rearrange your kitchen cupboards so the dishes are now where the coffee mugs used to be (and vice versa). Now, if you've got a little cash set aside for reclaiming your space, here are some suggestions for rocking your recovery. Start your own list here and finish it up in Worksheet 2 at the end of the day:

1. Replace a piece of furniture your ex took with something that's just your style.
2. Add a snugly new blanket, quilt, or throw to your fave nesting spot.
3. Invest in new wineglasses or dishes so that every time you eat or drink, you're not reminded of your ex.
4. Change the look of your entryway so that when you walk into your home, the image that greets you does not remind you of him.
5. Feminize your bathroom with pretty new hand towels, soaps, lotions.

6. _____

_____

7. _____

_____

BREAKUP RECOVERY TIP

 ### Get Rid of Ex-Boyfriend Bling

While performing your final ex-orcism today, you may come across some jewelry or other valuables your ex gave you once upon a time. Instead of getting sidetracked with a stroll down memory lane, check out *www.ExBoyfriend Jewelry.com*. You can buy/sell/trade your jewelry *and* blog about your breakup (so therapeutic!). They even have a place for you to donate the money you make from your ex-boyfriend bling to breast cancer charities. Breaking free from his memory *and* donating to a good cause? It doesn't get any better than that!

Reclaim Your Single Status

In addition to reclaiming your space, reclaim your single status in your home as well. How? Create healthy, happy visual reminders of who you are and who you continue to become as a result of the breakup. The following are some suggested ways to reclaim your single status throughout your home.

Build a Breakup Recovery Shrine

You don't have to be particularly religious or spiritual to create a shrine that's meaningful to you. Collect symbols of strength like a Buddha statue, fairy figurine, goddess art, candles, and/or inspiration words like *Peace, Love, Joy, Laugh*. Assemble your shrine in a corner of a room, on a shelf above a comfy chair, or in a spot left vacant by his stuff. Then sit, relax, and meditate in front of your shrine. You can even practice your gratitude list for the day in front of your shrine, starting with *I am grateful for reclaiming my single status today!*

Assemble Your Vision Board

In Week 1, I suggested you start collecting images for a vision board. The goal is to find images that reflect your bright future including what your dream home, ideal relationship, circle of friends, and passionate career look like. Once you've gathered plenty of images and inspiration words, get a thick piece of paper or cardboard, arrange the images and words in a visually pleasing way, paste them on, and hang the vision board in a place where you'll regularly see it. Get as creative and dreamy as you like!

Write down some inspirational words.

_____

_____

_____

_____

_____

Find a Symbol of Your Breakup Recovery

This is an exercise I introduced in my first book and continue to use with my clients. Sometime today or in the coming days, I want you to find a symbol of your breakup recovery. It doesn't have to cost anything or be elaborate. The goal is to place a visual reminder of your recovery somewhere in your bedroom so that it is one of the first things you see when you go to sleep at night and wake up in the morning. My breakup recovery symbol was a red feather boa that I hung on my bedroom door. It was fun, fabulous, and bold, always reminding me visually that regardless of the pain I was feeling in the moment, I was making progress. Regardless of how much doubt I sometimes felt, I *would* eventually heal and move on. Go ahead and find a symbol of your breakup recovery. Suggested symbols include:

1. Your breakup recovery calendar complete with gold stars
2. A framed photo of you and your Boo-Hoo Crew to replace the photo of you and your ex that used to be on your nightstand

3. Your newly created shrine including candles, inspirational quotes, and other symbols of your happiness and newfound freedom (have fun creating this!)

4. Fresh flowers that you buy for yourself weekly from now on (just make sure your ex didn't give you the vase)

5. Your work-in-progress vision board (keep adding to it as you find inspiring quotes and images)

Write down any other ideas that you have to symbolize your breakup recovery here.

6. _____

   _____

7. _____

   _____

Having a visual symbol of your recovery will help keep you on track during the tough times when all you really want to do is call, e-mail, or text your ex. (Don't do it!) Instead, focus on your recovery symbol, practice deep breathing, and remind yourself that you're doing everything right. Day by day, it's getting easier. Just keep going!

 ## Chapter *Check-In*

Reclaiming your space is about more than just getting rid of his stuff. It's about celebrating you—the beautiful, inspired, and empowered you who is emerging during your recovery. As you head for bed tonight, I hope it will be in a bedroom that is *what's his name*-free. From now on, my wish is that you love spending time in your bedroom. This is your most sacred space, after all!

And now for your nightly assignment: Take a look around your cleansed bedroom and ask yourself what new and happy memories you want to create in this room. Do you want to take up nightly meditations in front of your recovery shrine? Eventually bring someone new (and fabulous) into your life, and if he's worthy, into your bedroom? Only you will know for sure the new memories you want to create in your most sacred space. As always, give yourself permission to dream B-I-G.

And if being in your bedroom without your ex still feels a little painful, that's okay. This is a journey and there is no right or wrong way to feel at any given time. Practice patience. Don't forget to mark your recovery challenge calendar with that big fat gold star I hope you earned today. Then slide into the sheets and rest easy knowing that you did amazing work. Woo-hoo!

worksheet 1
reclaim your most sacred space

Make a list of things you can do specifically to your
bedroom to ex-orcise your ex. Do as many as you
can today and then commit to completing the list
in the coming days and weeks.

DATE _____

_____

_____

_____

_____

_____

_____

_____

_____

_____

_____

worksheet 2
reclaim the rest of your space

Make a list of at least ten things you can do to
the rest of your home to ex-orcise your ex (get
rid of his stuff, introduce a new scent, delete all
his favorite programs from TiVo). One by one, do
them.

DATE _____

_____

_____

_____

_____

_____

_____

_____

_____

_____

_____

_____

worksheet 3
visualize new experiences

Make a list of the new and happy memories you
want to eventually create in your bedroom, as well
as the rest of your home. Give yourself permission
to dream big!

DATE _____

_____

_____

_____

_____

_____

_____

_____

_____

_____

_____

_____

worksheet 3
visualize new experiences—*continued*

_____
_____
_____
_____
_____
_____
_____
_____
_____
_____
_____
_____
_____
_____
_____
_____
_____
_____
_____

DAY 11
the halfway
hump SLUMP

Today, I feel . . .

_____

_____

_____

Congratulations! Today, you've reached the halfway point in your recovery. I'm so proud of you. But more important, you should be proud of yourself. Healing and moving on from a breakup is hard work. There are no medals for just making it through the day, no recognized holiday for being a breakup survivor, and no official timetable for when the pain will subside. And yet here you are—a total rock star—taking it day by day, gold star by gold star, big red circle by big red circle. Before you move on to the second half of this journey, write down how you're feeling and acknowledge and celebrate all your efforts over the past ten days. In doing so, you'll see just how far you've come and why it's essential that you keep moving forward. If you find yourself in a bit of a halfway hump slump, don't worry. We're going to work through it so that you can not only dump your slump on Day 12 but look forward to your fabulous future. As scary as the unknown can be, it's so much more promising and loving than the past you've left behind. Let's get to work!

A Brief Check In

How are you *really*? I'd like to think you're feeling healthy, happy, and ready to move on with your life. But the truth is, I'm not sitting next to you or holding your hand. As far as I know, you could be experiencing a halfway hump slump, stuck in the post-breakup blues, unable, or unwilling to move forward. I'm *guessing* that you're somewhere between your old and new life, which is to be expected on Day 11. After all, your old life is still close enough that you can reach out and touch it, while your new life may seem uncertain and not yet attainable. Before you can dump your slump, you need to figure out just how attached you are to that old life vs. how you feel about the new future that's slowly unfolding in front of you.

Let's start by identifying where your focus is today. Are you fixated on the past; wavering somewhere between the past, present, and future, or firmly focused on your future? Find out by reviewing the following scenarios. See which one most resembles your recovery status today.

Signs You May Be Hung Up on the Past

Does the breakup still seem fresh? Do you spend much of your day thinking about your ex, what went down, and what *could've been*? Are you so consumed by your unanswered questions that it's impossible to think about your fab future? If so, then you're probably a little too focused on the past. Before you scold yourself for bad post-breakup behavior, listen up. You're not wrong for holding on to your past. It happens, *especially* if the breakup came out of the blue. Being blindsided by a breakup can leave you with a lot of unanswered questions, not to mention fear about the unknown future. In other words, it's okay if you're experiencing the halfway hump slump. It doesn't mean you don't want to move on. You just may not know how.

To successfully survive and thrive, you need to let go of your vice grip on your ex, your life with your ex, and all those darned unanswered questions. Later in this chapter and continuing into the next, I'll address the most common fears people have about dumping their halfway hump slump as well as how to feel the fear and leap into the great unknown anyway. For now, keep the faith and keep reading!

Signs You're Stuck Somewhere Between the Past, Present, and Future

When you close your eyes, how do you feel at the very core of your being? If you're wavering somewhere between your past, present, and future, it may feel as if you're standing on the edge of a cliff. If you look behind you, you can still see your past fading into the distance. If you look beyond the edge of the cliff, your future is just starting to take shape. The good news is, you're able to see the future in front of you. It may be foggy and unfocused, but it's there. It's up to you to take the leap of faith, dump your halfway hump slump, and dive into the beautiful unknown. The rest of the chapter and the next will show you how.

Signs That Your Focus Is on Your Fabulous Future

If you're incredibly brave and bold, you may have no desire to look over your shoulder at the past. Your ex? He's just some guy who enjoyed the pleasure of your company once upon a time, but is now long gone. As for you, you're so ready to dump your halfway hump slump and dive off that cliff! Today, give yourself permission to leap. You don't have to know where you'll land. Just have enough faith to know that you won't crash and burn. Instead, you're going to soar to new heights. Bravo, rock star! Just keep reading and kicking serious post-breakup butt.

Face Your Fear Factor, Part Deux

On Day 6, I told you that the difference between the people who barely survive their breakup and the people who succeed and thrive lies not in whether they *feel* fear after the breakup. It's how they *handle* the fear. It's only natural to be afraid to leave behind your old life, however painful, for a new life you know so little about. But, what if instead of looking at your new life as unknown and scary, you see it as exciting, full of possibility, and with the opportunity to experience love, happiness, and fulfillment beyond your wildest dreams? What if the unknown future is more joyful, more satisfying, more amazing than your painful past? The truth is, I *know* your future holds all of those things. But for you to achieve it, *you* need to believe it. First, you may need to let go of your future-based fears. To help you do that, I went in search of the absolute best advice on the subject of letting go of fear. It's my pleasure to share another expert's insights with you, especially one I have found so incredibly helpful.

I, too, have sought help at various times in my life. During a difficult period following my Big Breakup, I discovered the work of Dr. Barbara De Angelis, an internationally respected personal and spiritual growth expert. Through her program *Making Love Work*, I was able to understand and identify my fears about letting go of Mr. Ex and our long-dead relationship. I was also able to see that letting go wasn't nearly as painful or frightening as holding on to a past that no longer worked for me. By sharing Barbara's expertise with you in this chapter, I hope that you can face your fears of letting go so that you, too, can heal and move on to your beautiful future.

Based on her program, here are the four fears Barbara believes keep people from letting go of the past and leaping into their bright and beautiful futures:

Fear 1: Making a Mistake

What if you were to leap away from the life you've known and the ex you may still love, only to regret your decision? What if your new life was more miserable than the old one? Or worse, what if you took a flying leap away from your comfort zone and crashed and burned instead of landing on solid ground? The truth is that fear of failure can be powerfully paralyzing. If you let them, the *what-ifs* can keep you stuck *forever* in an old life that no longer works.

May I let you in on a little secret? The only mistake you can make at this point in your recovery is to stay stuck. You've already taken a huge leap. The breakup happened. You're still here. You're well on your way to surviving and thriving. As the saying goes, feel the fear and do it—take that leap—anyway!

Fear 2: The Unknown

What will it be like over there? What if I don't like it? These are common questions when you're stuck in your fear of the unknown. But guess what? Whether you did the dumping or got dumped, your past no longer works for you, and your present probably feels an awful lot like being stuck. The only person who gets hurt in this scenario is you. Everyone else, including your ex, is leaping into their blissful futures. Why not feel the fear, take the leap, and join your friends on the other side? You deserve to move on. And I promise you, you will survive and thrive!

Fear 3: Leaving Your Old Life Behind

Regardless of how happy or unsatisfied you were with your ex, there was probably comfort in knowing what your immediate future looked like. You most likely knew who you had plans with on Friday and Saturday nights, where you were going for the holidays, and who you could count on in a crisis. Now I'm asking you to leave all that behind for a life you know nothing about? You better believe it! As scary as it sounds, it's the only sane option. In other words, it would be insane to stay stuck.

Let me repeat that. Staying stuck in your old life and old ways is actually kind of nuts. After all, that old life doesn't exist anymore. Staying stuck in the past doesn't honor the amazing individual you are right now and continue to become, thanks to the breakup. Leaping into your bright and beautiful future is the only sane option available. But before you leap, you may need to dump any excess emotional baggage, ties to your ex, and any old behaviors and attitudes that no longer work for you. Think of it this way: You now have permission to let go of what no longer works in your life *and* to reinvent yourself as well. Go for it!

Fear 4: Losing Control

There's a little control freak in all of us (maybe even a big one!). Thanks to the breakup, your control freak is probably freaking out right about now. *What about all those plans you had with the ex? What happened to your day-to-day routine? This isn't control. This is chaos!* To put it bluntly, your control freak does *not* want to embrace any more change right now, which means that letting go and leaping are out of the question. But guess what? Change is a natural part of life. Losing control happens from time to time. Going through a breakup forces you to lose control *and* to face your fears about change and the future. Now's the time to face those fears and then release them so that you're able to let go and leap. I promise you this. You will not fall to your death. Instead, you are going to soar higher than you probably ever dreamed possible! But first, you gotta lose some of that control.

In reviewing the four reasons you might be feeling fearful about your future, were you able to identify which fear(s) currently hold you back? Regardless of which one resonated most with you, it *is* possible to release all your fears and take flight. To put it another way, why wait? What else has to happen before you take that leap? Do these ideas fit? If not, write your own!

o Do you need to sink deeper into your post-breakup funk?

o Do you need to drive all your friends away with your obsessive rants about your ex?

o Do you need to get a (*gulp*) marriage announcement in the mail from your ex, a clear sign he's moved on while you're still stuck?

o _____
_____

o _____
_____

Why not give yourself permission to let go and leap today? Aren't you worth it? I think so, but what's really important is that you think so. Yes, change is scary. Yes, old habits die hard. But it is harder and scarier to hold on to a past that no longer works, a past that has already moved on without you. And whether you know it or not, it has.

it's a
BREAKUP *not a*
BREAKDOWN
WORKBOOK

 Chapter *Check-In*

How are you feeling, *really*? I hope today you were able to determine where you are in your post-breakup recovery as well as identify any fears you have about leaping into your future. By dumping your halfway hump slump, you take one step closer to healing and moving on. Tomorrow, we'll dive into what might still be holding you back. By the end of Day 12, you'll have dumped all that excess baggage and be ready to take flight. What happens next is not only fun and fabulous, but it's all about embracing that bright and beautiful future you deserve.

And now for your nightly assignment: Put on some relaxing music, find a comfy spot, and close your eyes. Take several slow calming breaths to quiet your mind. Once the internal chatter dies down, visualize yourself on the edge of a cliff. Pay attention to what's below you (grass, ocean, rocks?). Then pay attention behind you as you become aware of your strong, exquisite, magical wings. Take another deep breath. Spread your wings and get a sense of their awesome power. When you're ready, leap off the cliff and take flight. Enjoy the sensation of wind on your face as you soar through the air. Take yourself on a journey into your future. What do you see, hear, and feel—joy, abundance, success, love, laughter? Maybe you see your future self—beautiful, strong, and completely over the breakup, living and loving your new and improved life. Pay attention to whatever comes to you. Keep breathing. Sit back, relax, and just enjoy the sensory experience. Take as long as you need. Don't rush this journey into the future.

When you're ready, come back to reality, landing safely. How did that feel? I hope you had a good trip and saw many amazing things in your future. You're now ready for a sound night's sleep and another day of leaping tomorrow. Don't forget to mark your recovery challenge calendar depending on how you did avoiding contact with your ex. Here's hoping it was another gold-star day!

worksheet 1
what's holding you back?

After reading about Day 11, were you able to identify the fears that may be holding you back from your fabulous future? Identify the fear here and write about how it may be keeping you stuck. If more than one fear applies, write about each one.

P.S.—You only have one worksheet today. That means it's very important to take plenty of time to identify and journal about your fears of moving on. Don't skip this step.

DATE _____

My greatest fear of the future is:

_____

_____

_____

_____

_____

_____

_____

_____

_____

_____

_____

Here's how it is keeping me stuck:

_____

_____

_____

_____

_____

_____

_____

_____

_____

_____

_____

_____

_____

_____

_____

_____

DAY 12
DUMP
your slump

Today, I feel . . .

_____

_____

_____

Welcome to Part Two of the halfway hump slump. While yesterday was all about identifying and facing your fears of the future, today we're going to take the next step and help you dump your halfway hump slump—for good! First, write down how you're feeling today. Next, you're going to identify what, if any, payoffs you're enjoying by staying stuck in the past (or wavering in the present). Then, you'll figure out what you may need to forgive yourself for following the breakup. And finally, at the end of this chapter, you're going to take a flying leap into your fab future. This is just the beginning of Part Two of your recovery journey.

The Pitfalls of Payoffs

Staying stuck in the past can be painful, uncomfortable, and downright disastrous. Yet you may choose to stay stuck rather than let go and leap. There may even be payoffs for holding onto the past. While there are plenty of payoff perks, there are plenty more pitfalls. In order to purge your past, you first need to identify what your particular payoffs for staying stuck are. Take a look at the following list of common payoffs. See which, if any, sound familiar.

Payoff 1: Avoidance

By staying stuck in the past following your breakup, you get to avoid all kinds of things. Check out the following or write your own!

1. Making necessary and important changes in your life
2. Taking responsibility for your emotions and future
3. Ever having to achieve any kind of success ("The breakup ruined me.")
4. Possibly getting your heart broken again (instead believing that it's safer to stay stuck than take another love risk)

5. Possibly finding the love of your life (What a shame!)

6. _____

_____

7. _____

_____

Payoff 2: Punishment

By staying stuck following your breakup and refusing to heal, move on, and find future happiness, who are you trying to punish? Your ex? Your parents? Your friends? By holding on to the past, you get to say, "See, you really hurt me. Look how damaged I am." It's as if the pain validates your existence while punishing the people around you. In reality, the person you hurt the most is yourself because you never get the chance to heal and move on. Ouch!

Payoff 3: Manipulation, or Emotional Blackmail

Playing the victim or the poor suffering martyr is a common post-breakup payoff. As a victim, if everyone feels sorry for you, you don't have to heal and move on. Besides, negative attention is better than none, right? Wrong! As a martyr, you may believe you're suffering silently, all the while expecting that everyone around you understands and sympathizes with your ability to endure so much pain. The truth is, sooner or later people tire of catering to the victim or martyr in their life. Rather than rely on sympathy and self-pity, wouldn't it be

so much easier to let go, move on, and become a true recovery rock star? (The answer is *Yes!*)

Here's the thing about payoffs. They're emotionally exhausting and spiritually draining, and they strip you of your dignity. You're far too fabulous to stay stuck. If any of the payoffs mentioned feel familiar, you owe it to yourself to purge and move on.

The Forgiveness Factor

Here's something else for you to think about before you can let go and leap into your fabulous future. I touched on it briefly in Week 1, and it's definitely time to revisit. It's a question that only you can answer.

Have you forgiven yourself for the breakup?

But Lisa, you might be saying, *what do I need to forgive myself for? I'm the one who got dumped. I'm the one who's in pain. What's there to forgive?*

And that's what we need to figure out. Starting today, and moving forward, ask yourself: *What do I still need to forgive myself for?* Regardless of who broke up with whom, or how the breakup went down, you may still be blaming yourself. By identifying what post-breakup self-blame you're projecting, you'll get a clearer vision of how to let go and leap. Here are a few examples of self-blame or you can list your own and add them onto your worksheet at the end of the day.

1. I couldn't make the relationship work.
2. I am yet again a relationship failure.
3. I said and did hurtful things.

4. I stayed too long, even when I knew the relationship wasn't working.
5. I ignored my ex's unacceptable behavior, and sacrificed my dignity.

6. _____

7. _____

4. I forgive myself for staying too long in a relationship that wasn't working, and I pledge to follow my gut in the future.
5. I forgive myself for ignoring my ex's unacceptable behavior, sacrificing my dignity, and losing myself in the relationship. I now know better and will do better in future relationships.

6. _____

7. _____

Sound familiar? Most people play the blame game following a breakup. Although blaming your ex is part of the recovery process, blaming yourself can be far more dangerous. That's why forgiveness is so important. If you can't forgive yourself for what happened in the past, you won't be able to fully heal and move on to your fab future.

Take some time right now to ask yourself what you might still be blaming yourself for following the breakup. Once you've made your list, review it, and then ask yourself for forgiveness. You can even create a new list that begins with *I forgive myself for.* and fill in the blanks. Take a look at these examples, brainstorm, and continue your list when you fill out your worksheet at the end of the day.

1. I forgive myself for not being able to make this relationship work. Truthfully, I did everything I could.
2. I forgive myself for going through another breakup, and I understand that this does not make me a relationship failure.
3. I forgive myself for the hurtful things I said and did, and I promise to do better next time.

Together, we will continue to work on forgiveness throughout the rest of your recovery. For now, all you have to do is be open to forgiving yourself. You deserve it, and you're worth it!

Dump Your Slump—For Good!

During your halfway hump slump, you may ask yourself, *How did I get here?* followed by *What happened to the life I had before the breakup?* These are natural questions. Nobody likes starting over, especially if you had other hopes, dreams, plans. But you know the saying: Life is what happens when you're busy making other plans. While you may have had one plan for your future, the universe (or God, the Goddess, your spirit guides, etc.) had another. So here you are, starting over yet again (or for the very first time). The past is the past. The future is, well, unknown. As uncertain as that sounds, it's where you're headed. And it's fantastic!

But to get there, you have to first let go. Right here and now, I want you to let it all go.

I know, I know. I've just asked you to do the impossible. If the task of letting go sounds daunting, don't worry. Here's how: Make a list (see the worksheet at the end of the chapter) of everything you're holding on to from your past. I want you to spend plenty of time with this list and be as thorough as possible. If you need guidance, here are a few examples of what you might be holding on to from your past or add your own:

1. My ex
2. My disappointment in what *could've been*
3. Those obsessive questions that keep me up at night
4. That picture-perfect life he promised me (but never delivered)
5. My identity as *what's his name's* girlfriend

6. _____

7. _____

Once you've made your list, review it. Then ask yourself how holding on to those things serves you. How is it helping you heal and move on from your breakup? The truth is it's not helping. In fact, it's hurting. I bet it's hurting a lot. I know you're in emotional pain, but you may also be in physical pain. By holding on to a past that no longer works (especially if you're holding on with a death grip), your body responds by tensing up. Take a moment to really feel what it's like to live in your body right this very minute. Is there tension in your neck and shoulders? Is that recurring headache back again?

Maybe your stomach, which has been tied up in knots since the breakup, feels especially uncomfortable today. If you're holding on to your past for dear life, how is your body responding?

Think about how your body would feel if you let go of that past. The weight of the world might fall off your shoulders. Your hands, which have been gripping so tightly, might relax. That knot in your stomach will probably loosen and even disappear. The truth is your present and future health and well-being are worth a hell of a lot more than your past.

Take a long hard look at the list of things you're holding on to from the past. Then close your eyes. Picture yourself gathering up these things. Then visualize placing them on a boat, plane, or other vessel, and when you're ready, set them free (or better yet, set them on fire!). Go ahead. Right here and now, take a deep breath, close your eyes, and set your past free. Maybe it sounds scary. Maybe you don't feel ready. Do it anyway. Your future is counting on your bravery.

Once you've set your past free, sit for a minute, eyes still closed, reflecting on what just happened. Whether you know it or not, you've just taken a giant step away from your past, turned your focus toward your future, and are now staring into the vast unknown. Congratulations! This is *big*. Now all you have to do is leap (more on that tomorrow).

Chapter *Check-In*

My Chapter Check Ins are usually where I give you some final loving and nurturing thoughts for the day. Today I'm going to mix it up and (possibly) practice some tough love. As you get into bed tonight, I want to address how you're *really* doing when it comes to contact with your ex. This is where I empower you to hold yourself accountable for your actions and your recovery. So, how's it really going? Are there a lot of gold stars on your recovery challenge calendar? Or is it a mix of gold stars and red circles? Or have you given up marking the calendar because you're still in contact with your ex pretty much every day? Only you know for sure. But as you look toward the second half of your breakup recovery, I want to be clear. If you've been diligent about avoiding any and all contact with your ex, you are an absolute rock star! Give yourself two gold stars today. Not only that, go online to *www.LisaSteadman.com/rockstar* to claim your reward. You've earned it!

If you've had some contact with your ex, I want you to strive for zero contact throughout the remainder of this twenty-one-day program. That's nine straight days without any phone calls, e-mails, text messages, or physical contact with your ex. I know you can do it. Just stay strong!

Now, if you've been in constant communication with your ex during the past eleven days, here's where the tough love kicks in. You know better, don't you? You also know that the only person you're really hurting is yourself. I challenge you to go cold turkey for the next nine days. That's nine days of no e-mail, no texting, no phone calls, and definitely no booty calls with your ex. I know you can do it. But what's important is that *you* know you can do it. Right here and now, I challenge you to suck it up and commit to going cold turkey. You can start by signing the accountability contract on the following page. Once you've made the commitment to yourself and your future, you're ready to move on to the next chapter.

If you can't completely cut off communication with your ex—if there are kids involved, financial matters to discuss, paperwork to sign, I get it. You can't go cold turkey. But you can establish and maintain new boundaries, only discussing what's necessary, and never permitting your ex access to your emotional recovery. I know it's hard, but you're stronger than you think. Keep the faith and keep going!

worksheet 1
accountability contract

To ensure that you have zero contact with your
ex throughout the remainder of this program, sign
and date this accountability contract.

DATE _____

I, _____ , being of sound mind and healing heart, promise to
avoid any and all contact with my ex for the remainder of this program, including:

- o No phone calls
- o No e-mail exchanges
- o No text messaging
- o No physical contact of any kind (and especially no booty calls!)
- o No driving by, stopping by, bumping into him at his home, work, or fave hangout
- o And absolutely, positively no cyberstalking

Signed: _____

Date: _____

worksheet 2
play the blame game

Because you can't move on from your breakup
until you play the blame game and forgive yourself, make a list of the things you blame yourself
for following the breakup.

DATE _____

I blame myself for:

_____

_____

_____

_____

_____

Now review and rewrite, starting with I forgive myself for:

_____

_____

_____

_____

_____

worksheet 3
let go of the past

Before you can heal and move on, you need to first identify what you're holding on to from the past.

Homework: Review the list, close your eyes, and picture yourself setting all of those things free. This is an excellent bedtime meditation. Give yourself plenty of time to set each and every item free so that tomorrow, you're ready, willing, and able to leap off the cliff of your past and into the amazing future before you. Good luck!

DATE _____

Things I'm still holding on to:

_____

_____

_____

_____

_____

_____

_____

_____

_____

_____

worksheet 3
let go of the past—continued

_____

_____

_____

_____

_____

_____

_____

_____

_____

_____

_____

_____

_____

_____

_____

_____

_____

_____

_____

_____

DAY 13
take a
flying LEAP

Today, I feel . . .

_____

_____

_____

Now that you've let go of your past, it's time to take that flying leap into your future. But rather than take a leap into the unknown all by yourself, why not leap with that fabulously fun and fierce girl your ex fell in love with? You know the one, the one who's evolving into someone more and more incredible by the day. Today, it's time to reconnect with her. Look in the mirror and just say hi. Ask her how she's doing. Find out what she needs in order to heal and move on. Write down how she feels today. Honor her needs and wishes. In doing so, you'll master the art of self-nurturing while getting back to the business of Y-O-U. Before you know it, together you will have leaped and landed safely and squarely into your bright future.

Say *Buh-bye!* Nature, *Hello!* Nurture

As you take that flying leap today, it's the perfect time to leave behind any residual self-loathing, self-defeating, or negative behaviors/beliefs you hold onto, and instead adopt more self-nurturing tendencies. Learning to nurture your healing heart will be one of the best gifts you can give yourself during your recovery. If this is new and unfamiliar territory, be patient with your progress. It may not happen overnight, but it will happen. The following techniques will help you embrace your inner nurturer.

Reconnect with Your Inner Child

When was the last time you talked to your inner child? Even if it was last week, last year, or sometime in the last century, today's the perfect day to reopen the lines of communication. Start by looking in the mirror and asking your inner child how she feels. Or, if the idea of talking to your inner child in the mirror makes you uncomfortable (it takes practice!), find a comfy spot, close your eyes, and invite your inner child to chat. See what she says. Find out how she's feeling about all this growth and change. That anger, betrayal, disappointment, and isolation you've been feeling recently may come from her. It's important to listen to and honor your inner child's feelings, whatever they may be. As awkward as this can initially feel, by reconnecting with this part of yourself, you practice a valuable self-nurturing exercise. Continue listening to and caring for your inner child throughout the rest of this program. If the idea of having a conversation with your inner child sounds absolutely preposterous, don't worry. There are plenty of other ways to nurture yourself. Keep reading!

Seek Professional Help

Yesterday, I invited you to set your old life free in order to slowly but surely embrace your new and improved life (no easy feat, by the way!). As a result, you may be experiencing surges of excitement, anxiety, uncertainty, or panic today. That's to be expected. If you're having adjustment issues, you may want to seek professional help. This can be in the form of a therapist, life coach, energy healer, spiritual guide, or any other modality that resonates with you. The kind of help you seek is not what's important. What's important is that you're wise enough to recognize if and when you need help, and you're strong enough to ask for it. If you need some guidance in finding the right kind of support, ask your friends for referrals or go online and do a search for services in your area. Remember, asking for help is not a sign of weakness. It's a show of

strength. So, if you need to, make an appointment with your professional of choice for an emotional, spiritual, and/or personal tune-up. Your *happily ever after* future will thank you!

Let Go of Any Remaining Discomfort

In the last chapter, I talked briefly about how emotional pain can manifest itself physically. If you're experiencing any physical tension, strain, or pain right now, it's important to address it and heal it before it becomes a chronic condition. So how do you do that? It really depends on the type of discomfort you're experiencing and how severe it is. For example, if you've got neck and shoulder tension, a relaxing deep-tissue massage should do the trick. If you've been plagued with chronic headaches since the breakup, you might want to consider making an appointment with an acupuncturist. If you feel an overall physical or emotional stagnation, you may seek the help of an energy healer. This topic is incredibly subjective and while I'm not an expert by any means, I have sought out various healing methods throughout my life, depending on what I needed at the time. They include massage, acupuncture, chiropractic, energy healing, homeopathy, nutritional counseling, and several others. I can't tell you which one will work for you. What's important is that you listen to your body, get the help you need and feel comfortable with, and heal any physical stress, strain, pain, or other discomfort as soon as possible.

Give Yourself Permission to Purge

If your body's having a bad reaction to your breakup (i.e., pain), don't consider it a sign that you're being punished for whatever happened

between you and your ex. The pain is not proof that you're a bad person, nor is it a lesson you need to learn from. It's simply a physical symptom that manifests from stuffing your emotions. The best solution is to stop burying your post-breakup feelings. To truly nurture yourself, it's important to learn how to purge your pain. So go ahead, have another good cry. Or, if you're done with the waterworks, kick, scream, yell, or have your way with a voodoo doll resembling your ex. Better yet, work all that emotion out through intense exercise, journal writing, meditation, or pillow punching. The key is to let it all out. In releasing your emotional demons, any physical pain or guilt you're experiencing will most likely subside, too.

Get in Touch with Y-O-U

The next step in celebrating this stage of your recovery is to get in touch with the most important person in your life, *you*. The truth is you were an amazing individual long before you met your ex. And the fact that *what's his name* is no longer in your life does *not* mean your fabulousness went with him. Today's the day to celebrate that awesome chick you used to be, while coaxing the supercool woman you're becoming out of her post-breakup cocoon. The following activities will show you how.

Finish Your Vision Board

Since today is all about leaping into your future, it's also an excellent time to complete your vision board. If you haven't even started, spend some time flipping through magazines, collecting images and words that inspire you. When assembling your vision board, be sure to collect things that represent your ideal home life, desired romantic relationship, ultimate career, as well as any other personal aspirations (run a marathon, meet Oprah, travel the world, etc.). Once you've collected enough imagery, arrange it on a large piece of paper or cardboard, affixing with a glue stick. Then frame and hang your vision board in a place where you'll regularly see it. Mine hangs over my desk in my office. That way, I enjoy the inspiring images and words on a regular basis and am reminded daily of what's important to me.

Write Yourself a Fan Letter

Ready to really rock your recovery? Write yourself a fan letter! As silly as it sounds, this is an excellent exercise in nurturing yourself. Be sure to include why you rock, why other people admire you, and what it is that makes you so incredibly amazing. The only person who's going to read the letter is you so make it as fun, funny, kind, and creative as possible. Here are some possible openers or you can add your own.

Dear Diva,
I know you're in the middle of a breakup, but you're the bravest (and coolest) woman I know! Here's why:

To My Most Amazing Self,
As your biggest fan, I just have to tell you the many reasons you rock . . .

Hey Wonder Woman,
I just wanted you to know how much I love you. Here's why:

For My Brilliant and Beautiful Butterfly Self,

_____

_____

_____

_____

_____

While the old you may not have been comfortable being kind and complimentary, the new you should be ready, willing, and able to celebrate the many reasons you're fabulous. So go ahead (see the worksheet at the end of the chapter). Write that fan letter and make it saucy, silly, or serious—you decide!

Add to Your Fabulous Factor List

A few days ago, I invited you to create your Fabulous Factor List (see the worksheet on page 91). Today, I want you to add at least five new things to the list. Again, this list is for your eyes only so include all the reasons you think you're fabulous, regardless of how ridiculous or wacky they may seem. Start brainstorming here or add these examples to your list:

1. *I'm fabulous because I kick butt at Scrabble.*
2. *I'm fabulous because I can touch my nose with my tongue.*
3. *I'm fabulous because I make the most delicious chocolate fudge brownies.*
4. *I'm fabulous because for the first time in my life I'm living alone (and loving it!).*
5. *I'm fabulous because for my ___th birthday I'm taking myself to Europe.*

6. _____

_____

7. _____

_____

8. _____

_____

9. _____

_____

10. _____

_____

If you can think of more than five things to add to your list, go for it! The more the better. Now's the time to celebrate the way-cool woman you were, are, and continue to become.

Chapter *Check-In*

How did it feel today to nurture yourself? Even if you felt resistance, I hope you pushed through it and embraced the idea that being kind and compassionate toward you and your inner child will rock your recovery. Tonight, I want you to make a list of easy and affordable ways you can nurture yourself on a regular basis. From now on, it's up to you to take excellent care of the precious woman reading this book. Maybe you're just waking up to your brilliance, or maybe you're still filled with doubt about your own innate fabulousness. Either way, now is the time to learn to nurture yourself. Use the following list for guidance on easy and affordable ways to do that very thing:

1. Meditate for five minutes every night before bed
2. Take my vitamins every day
3. Buy myself my favorite lotion and lovingly apply it to my entire body after every shower (make this a self-nurturing ritual and not just something you do without any thought)
4. Remove any repetitive self-defeating thoughts (like *I suck*) and replace with self-loving thoughts (like *I rock!*)
5. Instead of sitting in traffic and stressing, practice deep breathing and affirmations

By making these simple self-nurturing adjustments to your everyday life, you're going to get so much better at taking care of yourself. That's the key to a bright and beautiful future. It's not about having a perfect life; it's about treating your imperfect self with love and respect. As with anything in life, this is not something you can master and then forget about. You put it into practice every day, moment to moment, for better or worse.

So how are you feeling right now? You took a flying leap today. Not only that, you've already landed safely in the future. Congratulations! Put a gold star on your recovery challenge calendar. To reward you for your efforts, tomorrow you get to have some fun!

worksheet 1
write yourself a fan letter

Go ahead—write that fan letter, telling yourself
how much you rock!

DATE _____

_____

_____

_____

_____

_____

_____

_____

_____

_____

_____

_____

worksheet 2
add to your fabulous factor list

Add at least five more things to your Fabulous
Factor List that you started on Day 9. See page 91
for more info.

DATE _____

_____

_____

_____

_____

_____

_____

_____

_____

_____

_____

_____

worksheet 3
nurture yourself

Make a list of easy and affordable ways that you can nurture yourself. Throughout the rest of this program (and continuing throughout the rest of your life), do at least one nurturing thing from the list on a regular basis.

DATE _____

_____

_____

_____

_____

_____

DAY 14

PLAN A girl getaway

One of the best things about going through a breakup is the opportunity to reconnect with old friends. After all, boyfriends come and go but girlfriends are forever. Now's the time to celebrate your gal pals with a Girl Getaway or Ladies' Night Out. Of course, you may not be able to execute your girl getaway today, but you can at least start planning for the festivities. And since you're two-thirds of the way through your breakup recovery (Woo-hoo!), it's time to start celebrating your newfound freedom. Regardless of where you go or what you do, give yourself permission to be a little risqué. Wear something revealing. Flirt with a total stranger. Behaving inappropriately for a night can be so liberating. Bring it, Girl!

Create Your Guest List

Before I talk about suggested activities, I want to address your guest list. In order to honor your breakup recovery thus far and celebrate your continued success, it's important to invite only your super-supportive friends. See, at this delicate stage, you could still get blindsided by an unsuspecting frenemy. If you were to invite such a person to your girl getaway, she might unknowingly—or even purposefully—derail your efforts to get over your ex. That's why it's important to first identify who you are going to invite. When planning your guest list, consider the following:

1. Invite and consult with your Boo-Hoo Crew on the rest of the guest list.
2. Include only those friends who've been supportive of your recovery thus far.
3. If you feel obligated to invite someone, but your gut tells you *no*, listen to and honor your instincts.
4. Don't include anyone who might mention your ex's name at any time during the festivities.

Your girl getaway can be a small, intimate affair or a big, bold bash. Ultimately, it's up to you. However, keep in mind that you'll be throwing yourself a major Movin' On party in Week 3. For now, continue to focus on nurturing your healing heart and celebrating with friends who are loving and supportive. Now that you're clear about who to invite to your girl getaway, let's move on to planning the fabulous festivities.

BREAKUP RECOVERY TIP

℞ Reclaim Your Social Life

If you and your ex shared an active social calendar, reclaiming your social life is essential to your recovery. First, don't ask or expect your mutual friends to take sides. Rather, let them know that you understand they'll still have a relationship with your ex. Simply ask them to make time for you, too, and to do you a huge favor by never mentioning your ex during your get-togethers. Next, fill your social calendar with fun activities. And don't be afraid of the occasional Saturday night home alone. Enjoy the pleasure of your own company while watching a movie, working on a home improvement project, making yourself dinner, or indulging in a glass of wine.

Suggested Activities

If you and your gal pals are super busy and getting away for an entire weekend is out of the question, then a Ladies' Night Out will do the trick. The following are some fantastic ways to spend your evening.

Dinner and Dancing

When was the last time you went out dancing all night long with your girlfriends? Chances are it's been way too long. Not anymore! Now's your chance to shake things up by shaking your groove thing with your gal pals. Make reservations at a delicious dinner spot; then do your homework to find out what local nightspot has the best music, the cute guys, and delish drink specials. Then gather the girls, slip on a saucy ensemble, and dance the night away! Keep in mind that the focus of the evening is not on meeting cute strangers but on celebrating your suddenly single status with your friends. Of course, if you happen to meet a cutie in the process, flirt away! And don't forget to tip your sexy waiter or bartender 25 percent. If you're feeling especially bold, slip him your phone number, too. Remember, tonight's all about having fun!

Cocktails and a Chick Flick

If you're in the mood for a more mellow evening with your gal pals, arrange to meet at a swanky sipping spot for cocktails, followed by the latest must-see chick flick at the local multiplex. That way, you've got plenty of time for catching up on one another's lives before enjoying a laugh or two at the theater. While you're at it, don't forget the popcorn and chocolate. By sharing sweet and salty goodies, you split the calories and have twice the fun! After the movie, you can rendezvous at a nearby bar or lounge for one more cocktail (and to check out the eye candy) before calling it a night. Or, if you and your friends are up for it, you can head to the local gay club and dance till dawn with your new boyfriends. If you like, host a slumber party following the night's festivities. Just give yourself permission to forget all about the breakup and, instead, celebrate the new you that's slowly but steadily emerging. That's what Day 14 is all about.

Girls' Night In

Sometimes the most fun you can have with your friends is in the privacy of your own home. If you and your girlfriends are in the mood to kick back, relax, and catch up on your lives without breaking the bank, then a girls' night in should do the trick. Just be sure to have cocktail mixers, music, movies, and board games on hand. If you're feeling brazen, you could even throw a passion party complete with adult toys and accessories. Sites like *www.Booty Parlor.com* will help organize your party (they even send a Bootician to host the festivities!). Believe it or not, tapping into your passion with or without a man can help further extricate your ex from your memory. Love that!

If the girls want to spend the night, have a slumber party in your living room. Stay up all night watching movies, gossiping, and giggling. By celebrating the platonic love in your life, you release any remaining sadness surrounding your ex and, instead, focus on your fab friends. This is yet another way to practice gratitude during your recovery.

What movies are on the agenda for tonight?

_____

_____

Rent a Limo and Paint the Town Red

To truly reclaim your single-gal status, you may opt to paint the town a luscious blushing red—and to do it in style, rent a limo. That way, you and your girlfriends can party-hop all over town—the museum benefit, the restaurant opening, the hip and happening lounge—without having to worry about the designated driver. Plus, you'll feel like a total rock star making a grand entrance at each and every hot spot from the back of a limo. Just be sure you're wearing panties so the waiting paparazzi don't get a flash of your naughty bits!

Recommended Reading

Need some girl-getaway guidance? The following books are dedicated to the art of getting away from it all in glamour or gritty girl style:

100 Places Every Woman Should Go by Stephanie Elizondo Griest

Fly Solo: The 50 Best Places on Earth for a Girl to Travel Alone by Teresa Rodriguez Williamson

The 50 Best Girlfriend Getaways in North America by Marybeth Bond

Wanderlust and Lipstick: The Essential Guide for Women Traveling Solo by Beth Whitman

Suggested Girl Getaways

Of course, if you and your gal pals can sneak away for an entire weekend, that's even better. Choosing a destination for your girl getaway will depend on your mood and how you're feeling about the breakup. If you're still feeling a little bit vulnerable, then a pampering getaway may be just what the doctor ordered. Then again, if you're feeling single and ready to mingle, you may want to mix it up with other fun and friendly singles. The following suggestions should help you decide on your diva destination.

Spa Weekend

If your breakup has you craving a little TLC, then you and your gal pals should pack your fancy robes and slippers and slip away to a relaxing spa for the weekend. There, you can melt away any residual feelings about your ex in the sauna, steam room, and spa.

Suggested activities: Be sure to schedule a deep-tissue massage, fabulous facial, or body scrub to help you release any leftover unwanted emotions. While you're at it, a group manicure and pedicure session is the perfect setting for a gabfest. Go ahead—dish the dirt while getting pampered from head to toe!

What to pack: Bathing suit, robe, comfy clothes.

Las Vegas, Baby!

Ready to rock your breakup recovery? Then gather the girls and head to Vegas for the weekend. Nothing says "I'm over my ex" quite like slipping into a saucy cocktail dress and stilettos, partying at The Palms, and testing your luck at the blackjack table. Or, for a more mellow Vegas experience, sip cocktails poolside with your gal pals during the day and then hit a hot show or two by night. If you happen to find some cuties to flirt with while you're at it, go for it! After all, what happens in Vegas stays in Vegas. Plus, a little harmless flirting never hurt anyone. And it just might be the next step in exorcising your ex.

Suggested activities: Sip cocktails poolside while working on your tan, dance the night away in one of the many bass-thumping clubs, get tickets to a hot headliner show, test your luck at the slots or craps table, exchange your $20 bill for $1 bills and hit a saucy strip joint.

What to pack: Bikini, little black dress, comfortable walking shoes for day use, strappy sandals for nighttime.

What not to do: Engage in drunken rebounding, drunk dial your ex, spend the entire weekend crying into a jumbo-size fruity drink.

A Weekend in Wine Country

You don't have to be a grape connoisseur to enjoy a weekend in wine country. But if you and your gal pals are looking for a relaxing and sophisticated getaway, pack your bags and head to Napa, Sonoma, or the wine region near you. Do some research ahead of time to find a cute and cozy bed and breakfast to stay in, and be sure to ask around for the best wineries to visit. Most wineries have information about their wine tastings online. Some even offer discounts, so it pays to do a little research before your trip.

Suggested activities: Consider hiring a limo so you and your Crew can hop from winery to winery without worrying about who is driving.

What to pack: Your driver's license (because no matter how old you are, it's always nice to get carded!), a notebook to record the wines you like, an extra suitcase to lug your wine finds home.

Cruise in Style

Nothing says *sayonara* to your ex quite like setting sail on the high seas. Plus, if you still feel the need to create more distance between you and *what's his name*, then a weekend cruise may be the answer. Or, if you're up for meeting a new cutie or two, a singles cruise will meet your needs (rebound at your own risk!). Either way, consult with your girls, decide on a destination, and set sail for unknown adventure.

Suggested activities: Explore exotic ports, snorkel with the cute ship instructor, and enjoy the twenty-four-hour buffet.

What to pack: A bathing suit, a stylish floppy hat, sun block, Dramamine (for those unexpected queasy moments).

Beach or Mountain Retreat

If you're still feeling the urge to retreat during your recovery, then a beach or mountain hideaway is the girl getaway for you. A quick search on *www. HomeAway.com*, *www.VacationRentals.com*, or *www.vrbo.com* (vacation rentals by owner) will show you vacation rentals in your area of choice. Then it's up to you to gather the girls, pack your bags, and retreat to your dreamy destination.

Suggested activities: Catch up on your reading by the fireplace or under a beach umbrella, go for a long hike in the wilderness or walk along the shore, sit out under the stars at night and admire the vastness of the universe, enjoy the idea that you're very, very far from your ex.

What to pack: Hiking shoes or beach flip-flops, bathing suit or suitable hiking gear, a great book you haven't finished, and a journal to record your thoughts, feelings, and post-breakup epiphanies as they come to you.

Where do you want to go for your girl getaway?

_____

_____

_____

_____

_____

 Chapter *Check-In*

While you may not be able to embark on your girl getaway today, you can at least take steps toward planning the fab festivities. Believe it or not, making time for your girlfriends is essential to your recovery right now. Not only should your Boo-Hoo Crew be available to help you heal, but they should also be ready, willing, and able to help celebrate the fabulous you that's emerging. You may still feel as though you're in your recovery cocoon, but every day you take steps toward becoming a beautiful and brilliant butterfly. By planning and taking a girl getaway, you celebrate that inner butterfly and encourage her to take flight. So go ahead, Butterfly, gather the girls and fly!

Tonight, practice gratitude for the amazing women in your life. From your best friends to your sister to your mom, you're lucky to have loving and supportive ladies to lean on right now. Even if your support group is online, give thanks for them. They're an essential ingredient in your recovery.

Guess what else is essential to your recovery? Keeping that distance from your ex. So go ahead and mark your recovery challenge calendar with your gold star. Are you honoring your accountability contract? If not, you're only hurting yourself. And now that you know how to nurture yourself, there's no excuse for letting your ex back in your life. Be strong!

134

worksheet 1
let the girl getaway begin!

Plan your Girl Getaway / Ladies' Night Out, complete with invitations.

DATE _____

Who is on the guest list?

_____ _____

_____ _____

_____ _____

_____ _____

_____ _____

_____ _____

_____ _____

_____ _____

_____ _____

_____ _____

_____ _____

What is on the agenda?

_____

_____

_____

_____

_____

_____

_____

_____

_____

_____

_____

_____

_____

_____

_____

_____

_____

worksheet 2
plan future girl getaways

Make a list of future Girl Getaways / Ladies'
Night Out activities and destinations. Work them
into your single-gal plans in the coming months.
Now's the time to celebrate those fabulous female
friendships!

DATE _____

_____

_____

_____

_____

_____

_____

_____

_____

_____

_____

_____

_____

DAY 15
get a POST-BREAKUP
makeover

Today, I feel . . .

_____

_____

_____

Welcome to Week 3! Can you believe how far you've come in just fifteen days? How are you feeling? Fabulous? No matter how you feel, write it down and get it out. Remember, whether you know it or not, you're making remarkable progress. In fact, right about now you may feel as though you're hitting your stride. If so, congratulations! If not, don't worry. Either way, you're going to celebrate your resilience by getting a much-needed post-breakup makeover today. Go glam with a new cut, color, and highlights, a new wardrobe, or a whole new makeup bag chock full of glam goodies. By feeling fabulous on the outside, you're going to feel even more fab on the inside! In reinventing your exterior today, you'll be ready, willing, and able to focus your energies inward tomorrow, ditching any remaining unhealthy or self-destructive habits, beliefs, or behaviors. You will be making way for the fabulous new you—both inside and out. For now, it's time to channel your inner glamour girl with a fresh and fabulous makeover. (Are you on a budget? Keep reading. I've got plenty of cost-effective tips that'll have you rocking your new look in no time.)

Your Must-Have Makeover

When I started writing this chapter, I was somewhat surprised that I hadn't mentioned getting a post-breakup makeover sooner. But, the truth is, you wouldn't have been ready for it in Weeks 1 or 2. Back then, you would have taken one look at your new do, wardrobe, or makeup and sunk into a serious funk. You may have even contacted your ex to see what he thought of your new look. Guess what? Getting your must-have makeover has nothing to do with your ex. It's all about celebrating you and your amazing new life, which is why Week 3 of your recovery is the perfect time to go glam! Here are some fab, fierce ways to reinvent your exterior. You do not have to incorporate them all nor do you have to break the bank for a new look. The goal is to give yourself a makeover that inspires you to keep moving forward. In that spirit, let the transformation begin!

A New Do, a New You

Let's face it, Lady. You love your locks. As women, much of our identity is wrapped up in our short, sassy do, our mid-length waves, or our long, luscious tresses. If your ex had a thing for how you wore your hair, that's all the more reason to get a new Movin' On do. Your mane makeover can be as simple as going from one length to layers, adding a little vibrancy to your natural color, or getting highlights for the very first time. Or, if you're in the mood for a major makeover, go for it! For those who are ready, willing, and able to make a bold statement, try one of the following:

1. Go semishort and stylish with an angular bob in an eye-popping color.
2. Lop off your long dark locks for a short, spiky, blond look (you never know—blondes may have more fun!).
3. Channel your inner screen siren with a dramatic shade of red, auburn, or burgundy.
4. Take ten years off your look by getting super-stylish bangs.
5. Go punky glam with some colorful streaks (if you can confidently rock the look).

Whose fab hairstyle (a friend's or a celebrity's) do you love, but have always been too afraid to try?

_____

_____

_____

If you're not sure what kind of new do will work for you, talk to your hair-stylist, flip through hairstyle magazines, or ask your friends for input and inspiration.

it's a
BREAKUP *not a*
BREAKDOWN
WORKBOOK

Give Back While Getting Glamorous

Want to do something nice for others while getting glamorous? If you're chopping off ten inches of hair or more, donate your tresses to Locks of Love, a nonprofit organization that provides hairpieces to financially disadvantaged children who suffer from long-term medical hair loss. As I write this, I'm growing out my hair to do that very thing. If you've got hair to spare, I invite you to do the same! For more details, visit *www.locksoflove.org.*

Take Control of Your Closet

In previous chapters, I talked about the importance of getting rid of any items that remind you of your ex. If you haven't already, you'll want to do that today. Plus, now's the perfect time to open your closet, weed out what no longer works, and revamp your wardrobe. If the idea of taking control of your closet feels overwhelming, stop. Take a deep breath. Here's why re-working your wardrobe will rock your recovery:

1. Getting rid of any clothes that remind you of your ex can make you feel incredibly free.
2. A new outfit equals renewed self-confidence.
3. As you heal and move on from your breakup, you deserve to drape yourself in feel-good fabrics, bold prints, and vibrant colors.

4. Wearing fun, fab new clothes will inspire you to achieve other daring feats.
5. Slipping on a pair of new shoes can feel as though you're slipping into your new and improved life (Love that!).

Suffering from budget blues? Don't let financial woes hinder your closet control. The truth is you don't have to break the bank to rock a new look. Let me suggest a few ways to rework your closet on any budget. Feel free to add to it if you have some of your own ideas for reworking.

1. Tailor your fave somewhat-dated jacket, skirt, or dress for a modern fit; dye it a vibrant new color; or just add fun, funky accessories for a fresh look.
2. Take high-end items to a consignment shop and use the profits to buy new wardrobe pieces that make you feel super stylish.
3. Dig for hidden treasures at a thrift store.
4. Invest in a couple of classic new clothing items that you can mix and match for years to come.
5. Throw a clothing swap party, where friends bring clothes they no longer want and swap with one another (it's new to you!).

6. _____

7. _____

> ### Closet Control Cheat Sheet
>
> Follow these simple rules and you'll have a way cool wardrobe in no time:
>
> *Ditch and/or donate: Anything that does not fit or show off your shape, or in any way reminds you of your ex*
>
> *Keep/covet: Clothes that celebrate your shape, genuinely make you feel fabulous, and show off your sparkling personality*
>
> While you don't have to get an entire new wardrobe today, by clearing out your closet on Day 15, you engage the law of attraction. With more closet space, you're making room for the wardrobe of your dreams. Slowly but surely, you can restock your closet with pieces that make you feel beautiful, sexy, and confident. After all, the key to walking your new walk is to do so in feel-good fashions, fabrics, and footwear.

Just as cleaning out your closet will make you feel good, you can help others feel good, too, by donating your clothing. If you don't have a cause near and dear to your heart, the following are some organizations deserving of your designer duds:

○ Donate your professional attire (suits, dresses, accessories) to Dress for Success (*www.dressforsuccess.org*), a nonprofit organization that promotes the economic independence of disadvantaged women by providing professional attire and career development tools.

○ Donate any items of clothing to your local battered women's shelter. To find a shelter near you, do an online search. Be sure to call and get the donation drop-off address as they don't typically give out their physical location.

○ When in doubt, local churches, Goodwill stores, or homeless shelters accept donated clothes, shoes, and accessories.

Your Post-Breakup Makeup Makeover

Be honest—how many times a day do you look in the mirror? Even the most modest gal probably looks at herself (and judges her appearance) dozens of times throughout the day. How you feel about yourself is reflected to the world in your posture, the way you carry yourself, and especially in your beautiful face. If you don't feel fabulous, chances are you smile less, make less eye contact, and take fewer risks. That's why it's essential to schedule a post-breakup makeup makeover. To present your best self to the world, you need to feel beautiful!

Start by taking a trip to your local mall or department store, any store that has a variety of makeup counters. Although you may have worn the same brand of makeup for the last decade, it might be time to find a new brand, depending on your age. Spend some time browsing the makeup counters, asking questions, and paying attention to what makeup seems age appropriate. Whereas something cute and trendy works in your twenties, you'll want to rock a more sophisticated look in your thirties, forties, fifties, sixties, and fabulous years beyond.

Once you've decided on a brand, make an appointment with a makeup artist. These consultations are usually free with the hope of selling product. The beauty of seeking professional help is that you can talk about what you're looking for, get expert opinions, and then make an informed decision based on what works for you and your budget. Remember, it's not just about getting a pretty new shade of eye shadow, a sassy gloss for your lips, or guidance on where to brush on your blush. A true makeup artist can help you conceal those post-breakup bags under your eyes, find a foundation to smooth out blotchy skin, or find the right colors to make your inner beauty shine.

Once you've gotten your makeover, don't feel pressured to break the bank. Here are some cost-effective ways to go glam:

o Splurge only on high-end essentials like under-eye cream, the perfect foundation, and so on.
o Ask the makeup artist for a list of the products you like, and go online to find similar items at a discount.
o Compare prices at places like Sephora and your local drug store to get the best deal.
o Purchase one new item per paycheck so you don't blow out your budget.
o Be on the lookout for sales and special promotions on your must-have makeup items.

Rock Your New Look

Once your new look is complete, gather the girls for an impromptu photo shoot. Whether you're sipping cocktails and toasting to your new life, posing playfully on a makeshift catwalk in your home, or getting professional glamour shots done, let the inner you shine. Feel free to use these photos as you build your online dating profile in the coming week. However, they're mainly for you to replace any remaining framed photos of you during your relationship with *what's his name*. Even if he's not in the pictures, you may still identify your image as "his girlfriend." That's why replacing those old photos with ones of your gorgeous new self is yet another step in your recovery. Plus, by having visual reminders throughout your home of you looking super fly, you're going to realize just how strong and beautiful you really are. So go ahead, give yourself permission to rock your inner vamp. Put the pictures on your fridge, on the wall, and in your bedroom. You deserve to feel fabulous—today and always!

Chapter *Check-In*

Getting a glam new face, wardrobe, or mane may seem somewhat trivial and superficial. But the truth is, after a breakup it's only natural to feel down, including obsessing about your looks. You may even unconsciously blame your looks for why the breakup happened (*If only I were prettier, thinner, more like so-and-so*). That's why as you enter Week 3 of your recovery, a makeover is a must-do. You don't have to be a supermodel or make great money to rock a new look. Going glam has nothing to do with your body or budget and everything to do with reconnecting to your own personal fabulousness so that, in turn, your authentic inner beauty can shine. Besides, you deserve to feel like a glamour girl for a day, as well as in the weeks to come. Rock that new look with all your fierceness! This is just the beginning of your personal reinvention.

Tonight, I encourage you to journal about how your new look makes you feel. Be completely honest about all the emotions that are coming up during this process. Maybe you feel sexy, vibrant, and alive. But you can also feel freaked out, uncertain, confused. Remember, there is no right or wrong way to feel. By being honest about what you're feeling, you can get through it and eventually move on.

worksheet 1
go glam

As you get your glam makeover, chart your progress here. Be sure to include what you did (new hair cut, color, highlights, etc.) as well as how each action made you feel (beautiful, empowered, sexy, etc.).

DATE _____

_____

_____

_____

_____

_____

_____

_____

_____

_____

_____

_____

DAY 16
reinvent
yourself

Today, I feel . . .

_____

_____

_____

Okay, you've reinvented your look and become a total glamour girl. Now it's time to take that reinvention inward. Just as you let go of your old look in favor of a saucy new one, today you're going to ask yourself what other parts of your former self you need to bid goodbye. You're also going to assess what traits and qualities you'd like to embody as you become the most amazing, authentic you possible. Give yourself permission to dream B-I-G as you create and embody your fab new self. The only limits on who you become are self-imposed, so now's your chance to become a gutsy girl and go for it!

Let Go of Your Old Self

Your first order of business in taking a personal inventory is to ask yourself what aspects of the old you no longer work. Keep in mind that your mission is not to launch a personal attack on your psyche.

Rather, this is an opportunity to examine who you used to be and who you're slowly but surely becoming. Along the way, you want to identify any old behaviors, beliefs, or personality traits that may be holding you back (and need to be ditched immediately!). Things you'll want to leave behind include:

1. Limiting beliefs about love and relationships
2. Low self-esteem that inhibits your personal development
3. Deep-seated fears that forecast a bleak future
4. Walls or boundaries you put up to keep people out but ultimately leave you isolated and unhappy

By letting go of what no longer works, you take yet another step toward your bright future. So go ahead, ask yourself, _What about my past self no longer works?_

Make a list of at least ten things (see the worksheet at the end of the chapter). The more thorough you are in this exercise, the better. If you need help getting started, feel free to borrow from the following list, as it applies to you. Start brainstorming here and include your ideas on Worksheet 1 at the end of the day.

WHAT ABOUT MY PAST SELF NO LONGER WORKS?

1. I was too needy with my ex (and in every other relationship, too).
2. I couldn't be my true self around my ex and his friends.
3. I have a bad habit of throwing temper tantrums when I don't get my way.
4. I don't always follow through when I say I'll do something, and that bothers me.
5. I'm afraid I'm too screwed up to have a good relationship.
6. _____
_____
7. _____
_____

Once you've made your list, review it. Pay special attention to how many items on the list relate to your ex and how many issues you're still holding on to because you think there's still value in being defined by them or by him. For example, if "I was too needy with my ex" is on your list, are you still in a needy space, only now you've transferred your neediness to your friends (or worse yet, you're still needy with your ex, i.e., texting him twenty-seven times a day)? The truth is it doesn't matter who you were with *what's his name*. What matters is who you want to become now that you're free to be your most authentic self. This is one of the gifts your breakup gave you—the opportunity to become the real you. Love that!

Look at the list again. How many items relate to low self-esteem or limiting beliefs about what you deserve in life and love? There are probably at least one or two. Whether you know it or not, the only thing standing between you and the amazing life you deserve is your future belief system. Your past beliefs don't matter. Since you took your giant leap and left your past behind on Day 13, you've been free to create a brand spankin' new belief system. This new set of beliefs can be whatever you want and need them to be. You, too, can be whoever you want and need to be. The only thing stopping you is, well, you. Today, it's time to get out of your own way and embrace a healthy and happy new belief system that celebrates who you're becoming.

Embody Your Most Authentic Self

Now that you know that anything and everything your heart desires *is* possible, it's time to embrace your new belief system so you can embody your most authentic self. How? By digging a little deeper, of course! You can start by asking yourself the following questions:

1. Who do I want to become now that the breakup is behind me?
2. What does that girl look like?
3. What awesome qualities does she possess?
4. How can I start embodying those qualities today?

Take the time today (see the worksheet at the end of the chapter) to make a list of the traits and qualities you envision your most authentic self possessing. It's okay if the breakup still feels fresh or if you're experiencing resistance when it comes to embracing new beliefs. Do the exercise anyway, and give yourself permission to dream as big as you like. Let go of any fear or limitations. Remember, you ditched all of those limits when you took your flying leap into your future on Day 13. By mapping out the new and improved Y-O-U, you're making room to manifest these qualities, starting today. So go ahead and ask yourself: *Who do I want to become?* Take a look at the following list for inspiration and include your ideas on Worksheet 2 at the end of the day.

WHO DO I WANT TO BECOME?

The following are traits and qualities my most authentic self possesses:

1. I'm the kind of woman who attracts incredible, healthy, happy men.
2. I have an amazing ability to love myself unconditionally.

3. I possess an inner strength that allows me to easily overcome any adversity in life.
4. I exude a sparkling personality that draws the right people and connections to me.
5. I embody an adventurous spirit that inspires me to fearlessly go after whatever I want in life and love.

6. _____
   _____
7. _____
   _____

Again, give yourself plenty of time with this exercise. The more details you provide the better! In doing so, you create a road map of the person you're becoming. And don't forget to have fun. Creating your future self should be both empowering and inspiring. If it's hard or frustrating, stop. Look at your list. What about the list feels inauthentic? If you need to, crumple the list up, throw it away, and start again. This time, have fun! Feel free to include any visual traits your most authentic self possesses. For example, maybe she's got long flowing hair, is kinda buff, or maybe she wears cowboy boots. If the images come to you, include them. They're all part of your future self and that's fabulous!

Become That Gutsy Girl

Now that you've made a list of the traits and qualities that you'd like to embody, give yourself permission to become that gutsy girl. It won't happen overnight, but it can happen. You've just created the

road map. To arrive at your destination, you may need to conquer a fear or two. Now is the time to ask the next question: *What have I always wanted to try, but I've just been too scared to attempt?* Your answers may surprise you. Brainstorm here and include your ideas on Worksheet 3 at the end of the day.

WHAT HAVE I ALWAYS WANTED TO TRY, BUT I'VE JUST BEEN TOO SCARED TO ATTEMPT?

1. Skydiving
2. Speaking in front of a large audience
3. Getting a tattoo
4. Traveling to Europe solo
5. Changing careers / pursuing my dreams

6. _____

_____

7. _____

_____

By facing the things that scare you the most, you become clearer about what might be holding you back from becoming that gutsy girl. As you move forward, regularly review the three lists you just created (or will create at the end of this chapter) and ask yourself how you can become more and more like your authentic dream self. Challenge yourself to get outside your comfort zone if necessary to embrace the real Y-O-U. She's in there somewhere—it's up to you to celebrate her and bring her fully to life! To do so, you may need to face the things that scare you most. That's where that last list comes in. Regularly review it and add to it. Try to conquer at least one fear from the list in the next six months. By giving yourself permission to conquer what scares you, you may actually get excited about crossing more than one item off the list. You may even be inspired to cross everything off your list in the next year. Talk about becoming a gutsy girl!

Review Your Vision Board

Take a look at your vision board. What do you need to do to achieve that dream life? You've created the road map. Now it's just a matter of acknowledging the work involved and committing to taking the necessary steps. So go ahead, ask yourself: *What do I need to do to get to my dream life?* It's okay if the answers scare you. You don't have to take action today. But by asking yourself the question and answering it honestly, you'll become clearer about how to live your life moving forward. The following may be some of the steps you need to take to get to your vision-board future. If not, add your own.

THINGS I NEED TO DO TO GET TO MY DREAM LIFE:

1. Quit my job.
2. Stand up to my controlling parents.
3. Listen to and honor my inner artist.
4. Go back to school.
5. Move / get a roommate so I can save money.

6. _____

_____

7. _____

_____

As I said before, it's okay if some of the steps scare you. Change can be scary. But only with great risk comes great reward. And if you want to dream and live B-I-G (and I think you do) you probably need to make some changes to the way you live your life. You don't need to make all of the changes today, but you do need to acknowledge the work involved and commit to taking the necessary steps to get where you want to go.

Chapter *Check-In*

Are you feeling the momentum now? From your glam makeover yesterday to your personal inventory today, you may feel a lot of internal shifting going on. If that brings up some uncomfortable emotions, it's okay; don't avoid or stuff them. *Feel them. Celebrate them!* Laugh, cry, rage, rest—in doing so, you release any and all emotions without judgment, and give yourself permission to continue healing and moving on.

As you end Day 16, how are you feeling about leaving behind past behaviors, beliefs, and patterns that no longer work? This can be intimidating because I'm asking you to have faith that there's a better and brighter future out there for you. Whether you know it or not, a better and brighter future *is* taking shape. But first, it's up to you to let go of any remaining negative, dysfunctional, limiting beliefs and patterns that have held you back. You've already taken the big leap. The hard part is over. Now it's just a matter of embracing your new and improved belief system. Believing you deserve to be happy is the key to your success in Week 3. So, tonight at bedtime, work on that belief system.

Start by meditating on the phrase *I deserve a bright and happy future.* See if any resistance pops up. Let the resistance go and continue repeating the phrase in your mind. *I deserve a bright and happy future.* If it helps, say the words out loud. See how you feel when you loudly and proudly own the words *I deserve a bright and happy future!* If possible, bring a hand mirror to bed and repeat the phrase

to yourself in the mirror. As you fall asleep tonight, continue meditating on the phrase. Throughout the remainder of your recovery, you'll want to embrace the idea that *yes, of course, you deserve a bright and happy future!*

worksheet 1
let go of your old self

As you heal and move on, answer the following question: *What about my past self no longer
works?* Be brave and bold in your answers.

DATE _____

_____

_____

_____

_____

_____

_____

_____

_____

_____

_____

worksheet 2
embody your most authentic self

To get to that bright and beautiful future, ask yourself the following question: *Who do I want to become? The following are traits and qualities my most authentic self possesses:*

DATE _____

_____

_____

_____

_____

_____

_____

_____

_____

_____

_____

_____

_____

worksheet 3
become that gutsy girl

Make a list of things you've always wanted to do but never had the guts to try. In the coming weeks, revisit the list and give yourself permission to explore at least one item. Go for more if you can!

Regularly review these three lists in the coming weeks to chart your progress.

DATE _____

Things I've always wanted to do but never had the guts to try:

_____

_____

_____

_____

_____

_____

_____

_____

_____

_____

_____

_____

_____

DAY 17
shake UP
your routine

In the last chapter, you identified the traits and qualities your most authentic self possesses, as well as any changes you need to make to your current life to fully embrace your bright future. Although it may take time to implement those changes, today you're going to take that work a step further. You're going to shake up your daily routine in hopes of shaking loose any remaining bad habits or beliefs that no longer work for you. Today, you'll be testing your comfort zone, stretching it in order to make room for the new emerging you. Don't let that scare you. Give yourself permission to be brave and bold and test the limits of what's comfortable. You may be surprised to discover that the new you has already arrived. In the meantime, get ready to shake up your routine with the following activities.

Take a Speaking Risk

One of the best ways to shake up your routine is to take a speaking risk. What exactly is a speaking risk? It's any form of communication that challenges your comfort level in a good way. The following are some examples of speaking risks you may want to take as you shake things up moving forward.

Ask Your Boss for a Raise/Promotion

If you've been putting in long hours, performing above and beyond your job description, or simply believe you're entitled to more money, today may be the perfect day to ask for a raise. Or maybe there's been talk for some time about a possible promotion. If so, take a speaking risk and ask your boss about it. Don't be shy. Approach the subject with confidence. If necessary, state your case clearly and succinctly. When possible, give examples of how you're excelling at your job and why you think you deserve that raise or promotion. Then sit back, remain silent, and let your boss respond. If things don't go your way, stay calm and thank your boss for her time and get back to work. Then pat yourself on the back for being such a risk taker. If you score that raise or promotion, congratulations! Job well done. Regardless of whether or not you succeed, your boss will most likely respect you for taking a speaking risk. And the next time there's more money available? Guess who will be on her mind—Y-O-U!

Talk to That Cutie You've Been Eyeing

Have you been too nervous to approach that cutie you always see in the express aisle, at chiropractor's office, walking his dog? Take a speaking risk and just say hi. Be sure to smile and make eye contact when you do so that he knows you're interested. It doesn't have to lead to a date. You may not be ready for that. But, by getting up the nerve to strike up a conversation, you take an incredible speaking risk (and another step toward moving on). Go for it, Gutsy Girl! He may have been waiting for you to make the first move. You'll never know unless you take a risk.

Confront a Negative Friend

Is there someone in your life—a friend, coworker, or family member—whose negativity is bringing you down? From their *I told you so* attitude about your ex (or about men in general), to their Debbie Downer approach to life, having a negative person invading your space and polluting your attempts to be positive can be detrimental to your recovery. Today would be a good day to either confront this person or stop taking her calls. True, screening calls, texts, and e-mails is not exactly a speaking risk. But sometimes it's better to say nothing to these negative influences than to try and change their behavior. Only you will know the best approach to take. Either way, removing these downers from your day-to-day life will make moving on that much easier (not to mention a lot more fun!).

Stop Saying Yes When You Really Mean No

Be honest. Are you a people pleaser? Have you spent much of your life trying to be agreeable, saying yes when you really mean no just so you don't rock the boat? If so, then you owe it to yourself on Day 17 to put an end to this self-defeating behavior. Today, as uncomfortable as it may feel, give yourself permission to stop trying to please everybody. When somebody asks for a favor and

it's a
BREAKUP *not a*
BREAKDOWN
WORKBOOK

155

you don't want to do it, politely, but firmly say no. If somebody asks for your opinion and you would normally tell them what you think they want to hear, summon up the inner strength to kindly, but confidently tell them what you really think. Initially, this may be uncomfortable for both you and the people around you who are used to your old behavior. But you know what? Too bad! This is your life, and what's most important is that you're true to yourself, starting today. It may take practice, but if you're consistent in standing up for yourself, people will respond consistently. They'll either stop asking for your opinion or help, which is perfectly fine. Or they'll seek out your opinion because they truly respect it. Hey, that works, too!

Negotiate a Price

Want to take a really big speaking risk? Try negotiating a lower price on goods or services. (If this speaking risk scares the crap out of you, you should definitely try it!) And no, you don't have to go to a car dealership to haggle. You can negotiate a price on all kinds of things, including:

o Contractor work for your home or office
o Car repairs
o Vacation rentals and other amenities
o Professional services such as career or life coaching, graphic design work, accounting services

The point of this speaking risk is not to be cheap or to devalue someone's work. The goal is to learn how to start asking for what you want. If you never ask, you'll never get it. Today's the perfect day to train yourself to actively ask for what you want.

What speaking risks can you take? Brainstorm here and continue this exercise in Worksheet 1.

_____

_____

_____

_____

Become a Do-Gooder for a Day

Throughout this book, I've offered tips and ideas for rocking your recovery while giving back to others. Whether it's donating your ex's stuff to charity, taking closet control and giving to a needy cause, or chopping your hair during your glam makeover and donating your locks to less fortunate kids, there are plenty of ways to help the world around you while still helping yourself. But what if you could shake up your routine while doing something truly meaningful? Today, start thinking about how you'd like to help your community or a cause near and dear to your heart. The following are just a few ways you might want to consider giving back as you shake things up.

Give More than What Is Comfortable

Giving away old clothes and your ex's stuff is pretty easy. But what would it feel like to give more than you were comfortable giving? The truth is it would probably feel pretty fantastic. It might even help you stop focusing on your broken heart and, instead, open your eyes to the pain and suffering in the world around you. Yes, you loved and lost and it hurts. But some people have lost so much more—

their homes, their loved ones, their health—and they could really use your help. Here are just a few of the causes worthy of your support.

1. Relief funds for victims of natural disasters
2. A local family in your community who's struggling with poor health, homelessness, unemployment
3. Families of American service personnel killed in the line of duty
4. Victims of domestic violence
5. Animal rights organizations

For more info on a particular cause, do an online search and check out their website. Once you've found a meaningful cause that speaks to you, write out a check for more than you'd normally consider giving. And if you're fortunate enough to live well within your means and have disposable income left over, consider giving on a regular/monthly basis. You'll be doing a good deed for others and in the process feel fabulous!

Volunteer Your Time

While writing a check to a charity may make a dent in your wallet, it's not that large a sacrifice in the grand scheme of your life. Another way to give big is to volunteer your time. As busy as you may think you are, as valuable as your time really is, there's no greater use of your time than when you're giving it to someone or something in need. Suggested ways to volunteer your time include:

1. Mentoring a child after school or on weekends
2. Visiting chronically ill patients in the hospital
3. Spending one weekend a month helping a local animal rescue organization with pet adoption day
4. Donating a few hours a week at a local soup kitchen

Volunteering your time also helps you get out of that post-breakup funk because you're filling your free time with meaningful and positive activities that in no way remind you of your ex. Talk about a win-win!

Do Something Nice for Someone Else

Maybe you don't have much free time on your hands or a surplus of cash. That doesn't let you off the hook when it comes to helping others. The following random acts of kindness require very little time or money.

1. Buy and deliver flowers to the members of your Boo-Hoo Crew as a thank-you for being there during your breakup.
2. Call up a friend who is going through a difficult time and ask how you can help.
3. Help a disabled person safely across the street, carry his or her grocery bags, or offer some other form of assistance.
4. Offer to baby-sit for your married-with-child friend so she can have an afternoon to herself.

Helping other people does wonders for your soul as well. As you shake up your routine today, I hope you'll consider doing something good for someone else. Even if it's just a few hours of your time or a few dollars out of your bank account, every little bit helps—both them *and* you!

How can you help others? Brainstorm here and continue this exercise in Worksheet 2.

_____

_____

_____

_____

_____

Try Something New

Okay, you've taken a speaking risk and done something nice for someone else. Before we move on to Day 18, I've got one more suggestion for how to shake up your routine. It's simple, fun, and may just challenge your comfort level. I want you to try something new today. What exactly does that mean? It means whatever you want it to! Maybe you'll cross an item off your *Things I've always wanted to do but never had the guts . . .* list on page 153. Or maybe you'll take up a new hobby to help fill all that free time you've got now that *what's his name* is no longer in your life. Or maybe you'll recruit your gal pals to embark on another girl getaway. The following are some suggested ways to try something new. Borrow from the list or use your ideas to fill in Worksheet 3 at the end of the chapter.

1. Take up inline skating (or snowboarding).
2. Learn a new language (enroll in a class at your local community college or use an online program like Rosetta Stone).
3. Make an appointment with a financial planner and map out a retirement savings plan (and start saving today).
4. Grab the girls and go salsa, swing, or line dancing.
5. When you get home from work, instead of becoming a couch potato spend the next hour shaking your groove thang to your fave music (talk about shaking things up!).

6. _____

_____

7. _____

_____

Chapter *Check-In*

In case you're wondering, the importance of shaking up your routine is to remind you how fun and freeing life can be after a breakup. It's also a great opportunity to find new, healthy ways to fill the time you used to spend with your ex. Plus, it pushes your comfort zone and that's an essential step in embracing the new you. As for helping others, nothing makes a newly single gal feel better about herself and her fab new life than doing something selfless for a good cause. By becoming a feel-good philanthropist, you're that much closer to saying *buh-bye* to any remaining breakup blues and *hello* to your *happily ever after* future!

If you feel resistance to or are challenged by the suggested activities in this chapter, all the more reason to push your limits and try them. Be sure to celebrate your success once you shake up your routine. Tonight, have a glass of wine, treat yourself to some decadent chocolate, or take yourself to a movie. Also, be sure to give yourself a gold star on your recovery challenge calendar. By rewarding your efforts, you make moving on not just something you *have* to do but something you want to do. And that increases your chances of success. Rock on!

worksheet 1
take a speaking risk

Identify a least one speaking risk you can take
today or in the coming days. Once you've taken
the risk, record your successes or setbacks here.

DATE _____

My speaking risk is:

_____

_____

The results of my speaking risk were:

_____

_____

_____

_____

_____

_____

_____

_____

worksheet 2
do something nice for others

Make a list of ways you can do something nice for other people or organizations you'd like to help. Then see to it that you help at least one person or organization in the near future.

DATE _____

_____

_____

_____

_____

_____

_____

_____

_____

_____

_____

worksheet 3
try something new

Make a list of five to ten ways you can shake up
your routine by trying something new. Do at least
one thing today. In the coming weeks, add to the
list and cross off items as you accomplish them.

DATE _____

_____

_____

_____

_____

_____

_____

_____

_____

_____

_____

DAY 18
start a **healthy**
new HABIT

Today, I feel . . .

_____

_____

_____

At the very beginning of this book, I told you that conventional wisdom says it takes twenty-one days to start, create, or change a habit. As you reach the finish line later this week on your healthy new habit—that is, life without your ex—it may be time to focus your energies on creating a brand-new healthy habit. Since the split you've been getting stronger by the day. While your heart may be far from healed, it's well on its way to a full recovery. Write down how you're feeling and realize that today, you're gonna rock your recovery even harder by identifying another habit you have that no longer works for you. Whether it's changing your junk food / emotional eating regimen to a diet of more leafy greens and organic meats, joining or getting back to the gym, *finally* kicking your cigarette fix, or learning to practice positive affirmations, introducing a healthy new habit will take you one giant leap closer to your fab future. Love that!

Choose Your Healthy New Habit

As soon as I mentioned creating a healthy new habit, did something spring to mind? If so, fantastic! You're ready to rock-and-roll. However, if not, no worries. The following are some suggested bad habits you may want to kick, starting today.

Quit Smoking

While bad relationships can be toxic, an addiction to nicotine is seriously toxic to your *happily ever after* future. If you're guilty of puffing on cancer sticks several times a day, you owe it to yourself and your bright future to kick the habit, starting right now! If you've tried and failed to quit before, today's the day to try, try again. Think of it this way: As you continue healing your broken heart, you can heal your lungs as well. Plus, by giving up smoking, you increase your chances of attracting a nonsmoker. Talk about a healthier and happier future!

I didn't say it would be easy, did I? By definition, smoking is an addiction. If you need help kicking your bad habit, the following are some suggested antismoking aids. Have other ideas? Jot them down below.

1. Start wearing a nicotine patch to wean you off your addiction.
2. Try hypnosis to kick your nicotine cravings.
3. Buy and start chewing nicotine gum.
4. Join a antismoking support group (instead of lighting up, pick up the phone and call someone to talk you out of taking another puff).
5. Take up knitting, baking, or journaling to keep your hands busy (and your mind off the ciggies!).

6. _____
   _____

7. _____
   _____

Start Exercising

Packing on a few pounds at the end of a relationship or during your breakup recovery is perfectly natural. But rather than let five harmless pounds become ten or even twenty pounds of excess breakup baggage, nip your love handles in the bud by committing to a healthy new exercise plan today. If you don't think you have what it takes to hold yourself accountable, you'll want to get a support system in place. Here's how to enlist a little help in kicking your fabulous booty into shape:

1. Hire a personal trainer to tailor an exercise program to your specific needs.
2. Purchase a series of yoga or Pilates sessions and get your Zen on in a group setting.
3. Invite a friend to be your workout buddy (just be sure you hold each other accountable rather than enable each other to slack off).
4. Join a hiking group like the Sierra Club and get your butt in shape outdoors.

Creating a new exercise program at this stage in your recovery is a fantastic healthy new habit. Not only are you doing something good for your body, but the results will make you feel fabulous and you may just start attracting cuties left and right. Plus, by engaging those endorphins, you'll feel empowered, inspired, and forget all about *what's his name*. So go ahead, Girl. Move that body!

Eat Healthier

Whether you've been feeling sluggish since the breakup, want to drop a few pounds, or need to doctor your diet in some way, today's the day to make those nutritional changes. Take the suggestions below or add your own way to rock your eating habits.

1. Give up meat altogether and become a vegetarian or vegan.
2. Get tested for food allergies and give up whatever you're sensitive to.
3. Cut out excess carbs and sugar (you'll slim down in no time!).

4. Take a short- or long-term booze break, as needed.

5. Say *sayonara* to pesticides and buy organic produce, meats, and other food items.

6. _____

_____

7. _____

_____

Go Green

Chances are, you already recycle, right? But there are so many other ways you can be good to Mother Earth. To get you started on a greener path and reduce your carbon footprint, consider the following or add your own fantastic ideas.

1. Whenever possible, use public transportation and/or carpool.

2. Start composting (do an online search to find out how).

3. Replace your energy-zapping light bulbs with energy-efficient ones.

4. Trade your gas guzzler for a more fuel-efficient vehicle, hybrid, or Smart Car.

5. Buy organic foods whenever possible (organic farming is much better for the earth).

6. _____

_____

7. _____

_____

Start Being Nicer to Yourself

Whether you know it or not, you probably think, believe, and/or say terrible things to yourself from time to time throughout the day. Starting today, pay attention to both the internal and verbal messages you regularly give yourself. For example, when you look in the mirror, what do you think to yourself? Do you focus on the negatives (i.e. your bad skin, thick thighs, flabby arms)? If so, try changing the messages you send yourself. Whenever you look in the mirror from now on, first find something you like about your appearance. Compliment yourself. Maybe you're having a great hair day. Or maybe your outfit is super cute. Or maybe you got plenty of rest last night and your skin looks particularly fresh. By focusing on the positive, you change the way you communicate internally, which in turn changes the way you present yourself to the world. By being nicer to yourself, you become more confident, and project a healthier self-image.

Next, think about all the ways you communicate with yourself throughout the day. For example, how do you treat yourself when you make a mistake or feel embarrassed? Do you beat yourself up indefinitely or are you able to laugh at yourself and move on? Or when you eat something super indulgent like a pint of Ben & Jerry's or binge on your fave salty snack, are you able to really enjoy it or do you berate yourself for being weak, or worse, call yourself derogatory names like *Fatso*? Start paying attention to your internal words, beliefs, and actions. You may be startled to discover how frequently you berate, belittle, or insult yourself. Today's the day to not only stop being cruel, but to start being kind.

Here are just a few examples of new messages you can send yourself—starting today—that will make your life a whole lot more enjoyable and fun:

1. When you first wake up in the morning, instead of dreading getting out of bed, tell yourself it is going to be an amazing day, throw those covers back, and genuinely feel excited about the possibilities.
2. When you make a mistake, instead of beating yourself up endlessly, give yourself permission to stew for exactly five minutes, then forgive yourself and get on with your day.
3. When you're in a dressing room, instead of criticizing your reflection in the mirror, first find something fabulous that you like about your body (your bodacious booty, hourglass figure, fantastic tatas, etc.) and celebrate that body part with a little booty-shaking dance.
4. If and when you get rejected by a guy, don't blame yourself or beat yourself up. Instead, tell yourself it's his loss and that he's just made room for some other amazing guy to come into the picture in the future.
5. When something bad happens to you, instead of telling yourself that you're destined for misery or unhappiness or that you deserve to suffer, accept the bad news with grace, allow yourself to feel bad for a few minutes (or longer if needed), and then move on with your day.

Learning to treat yourself with kindness and compassion takes practice. But it's one of the best gifts you can give yourself because it shows other people how to treat you. By being nice to yourself, you engage the law of attraction. In response, others will start being kinder to you, too.

Find New Fave Places

Here's another healthy new habit to start today. Make a list of places you used to frequent with your ex. Rather than worry about running into him at any of those old haunts, do yourself a favor and find some new fave places to frequent. I know what you're thinking. Why should your ex get custody of all your former favorite places? Truthfully, neither you nor I can control where your ex decides to hang out. All we can control is where you choose to spend your free time in your fab future. And let's get real—running into your ex at this stage in your recovery? Not a good idea (especially if you haven't showered and he's with someone new). So go ahead, make a list of places you need to replace. The more thorough you are, the better. To help you get started, the following is a list of places you might need to replace:

1. Your weekend breakfast spot
2. The grocery store
3. Wherever you get your caffeine fix
4. The gym (or at least change the time of day you work out, to avoid a sweaty encounter)
5. Your favorite bar

List some new places you've been dying to try, but haven't gotten around to. Make it a point to try these places over the next few weeks.

it's a
BREAKUP *not a*
BREAKDOWN
WORKBOOK

_____

_____

_____

_____

_____

While it might not seem fair that you have to give up some of your fave places along with your relationship with your ex, the reality is that in order for you to really and truly move on, you're going to have to make some changes to your life. Besides, as exciting as the idea of running into your ex while you look super cute can be, you're more likely to bump into him when he looks hot (and possibly with a hottie on his arm) and you're a freakin' mess. It's just the cold, hard truth. The sooner you accept it and deal with it, the better. Do yourself and your recovery a favor and replace those fave places.

 Chapter *Check-In*

Congratulations! You've just committed to kicking another bad habit—for good! Whether you decided to give up smoking, start a healthy new eating habit, or get your beautiful booty into shape, I hope you feel inspired and empowered right now. You're doing everything right. Even if you're thinking about your ex right this very second, you're still rocking your recovery. And that's worth two gold stars!

Speaking of gold stars, have you been tracking your progress on your recovery challenge calendar? In Week 3, you're should be avoiding any and all contact with your ex, including screening his calls and texts and deleting his e-mails if he's still bothering you. Let's hope that by now he's got the idea that you're off-limits.

Here's something else to celebrate. In just three more days, you will have successfully completed your twenty-one-day recovery program. How awesome is that?! Whether you're feeling fabulous today or down in the dumps, take the time before bed tonight to give yourself a mental high-five. Seriously, Sister. You deserve a big smooch from the universe. Consider yourself smooched. Now get some rest. Tomorrow's another action-packed day.

worksheet 1
start a healthy new habit

Make a list of at least three healthy new habits
you'd like to incorporate in the next six months.
Start a new habit each month.

DATE _____

_____

_____

_____

_____

_____

_____

_____

_____

_____

_____

_____

worksheet 2
replace your fave places

Make a list of the places you used to frequent with your ex that you need to replace with new favorites. One by one, start frequenting the new places. Recruit your Boo-Hoo Crew for support, as needed.

DATE _____

_____

_____

_____

_____

_____

_____

_____

_____

_____

_____

_____

DAY 19
enroll in
SINGLE U

Today, I feel . . .

_____

_____

_____

While it may be too soon to start searching for your next great love (or even to start dating again), it's never too early to learn the ABCs of successful singlehood. But with just a few days left in your recovery journey, today's a great day to enroll in your Single University crash course. The following overview identifies a variety of activities that will, I hope, make your entry back into the dating world easy and fun, when the time is right. For now, sit back, read, enjoy, and write down how you feel. Plus, at the end of this chapter, I'll give you a super-secret link to your very own Single U download on my website. Class is now in session!

Ditch Your Post-Breakup Blinders

I've got great news! While you may have spent the last two and a half weeks obsessing about your ex, there are plenty of other guys to go gaga over in your future. When you're ready to get back out on the dating scene, your first order of business is to ditch your post-breakup blinders, and pay attention to the men in your everyday life. No, they won't all be available, nor will they all necessarily be interested in you (and vice versa). But, by noticing just how many intelligent, interesting, and attractive members of the opposite sex float in and out of your peripheral vision on a daily basis (on the subway, walking down the street, in the elevator, sitting in traffic, etc.), you'll discover that the possibilities are endless. Plus, you won't buy into the scarcity myth that so many singles suffer from that says there are no good men out there. There are plenty of good men out there! It's just up to you to pay attention. When you're ready, take off those blinders and see the men in your everyday life.

Break Free of Bad Love Habits
In Week 1, I touched briefly on the importance of breaking free of bad love habits and limiting

relationship beliefs. Now that you're so much farther along in your recovery, it's time to revisit this topic. In fact, as a student of Single U, your *happily ever after* future depends on your ability to embrace positive, life-affirming, feel-good beliefs about love and relationships.

Here's your assignment. Start thinking about any negative beliefs about love or relationships that you still have. Here are some to get you started or include your own negative beliefs on this list!

1. Everyone eventually leaves me.
2. I'm a failure at love.
3. I'm unworthy of love.
4. The only kind of love I deserve is painful, challenging, unsatisfying.
5. I'm doomed to be alone for the rest of my life.
6. _____
   _____
7. _____
   _____

Write down the ones that resonate with you. Then, reframe those negative beliefs with positive ones. They may include any or all of the following:

1. I deserve real and lasting love.
2. Relationships are satisfying, fulfilling, authentic.
3. Love is here, happy, passionate.
4. I attract the most amazing and healthy men.

5. I welcome healthy and happy love into my life.
6. _____
   _____
7. _____
   _____

Once you identify the new beliefs that work for you, try the following exercise: Repeat your new beliefs out loud every morning and every night for the next thirty days. It's a small time commitment that delivers big results. You'll be surprised how, in just a few weeks, your beliefs about love and relationships will dramatically shift. For more details on letting go of limiting love beliefs, visit *www.BadLoveNoMore.com*. To download a free audio introduction to my Bad Love No more program, visit *www.LisaSteadman.com/BadLovemp3*.

Earn Your Flirting Degree

Once you're ready to put yourself out there on the dating scene, you'll want to earn a degree in flirting. It can be fabulously fun, and doesn't have to lead anywhere. Has it been a while since you engaged in a flirt fest? Here's how to get started:

1. Find a flirting target (i.e. that cutie in line in front of you at the post office, at the bank, or while waiting to pick up your dry cleaning).
2. Make eye contact, and then look away.
3. Make eye contact again and smile.

4. If the cutie returns your smile, keep his gaze and say hello.
5. If this invites conversation, relax, smile, and enjoy (if not, move on to your next target).

Flirting really *is* that simple. You don't have to wear a tight sweater, hang out at a skeevy nightclub, or plaster tons of makeup on your gorgeous face to get a guy's attention. Truthfully, single guys are usually looking for a reason to talk to a cute girl. If you give them an opener, they'll take it. If not, don't take it personally. Maybe they just lost their job, found out they have two weeks to live, or worse yet, are emotionally unavailable. In any event, consider yourself lucky that they're not wasting your time and move on with your fabulous day. Nothing ventured, nothing gained!

Get Back Out There

Now that you're schooled in flirting basics, it's time to put yourself out there. By "out there," I mean in target-rich environments. As a relationship coach, I'm a firm believer in putting yourself in target-rich environments on a regular basis. It's your best chance of meeting like-minded individuals. So what exactly is your ideal target-rich environment? It all depends on your interests. To give you an idea of what might be the perfect environment for you, take a look at the following suggestions.

○ If you like live music, you'll want to frequent small music venues featuring live acts you enjoy. By choosing smaller venues, it's easier to scan the crowd, mingle, and meet other (cute) live music fans.

○ If you're passionate about art, scour the community guide in your local newspaper for upcoming art shows, museum benefits, and so on. Try to attend at least one art-related function a month. While you're there, talk to at least three strangers of the opposite sex. Practice makes perfect! Even if they're not available, they may have cute single friends who are!

○ If you love the outdoors, join an outdoor-centric group like the Sierra Club and regularly attend their organized events. Even if you never make a love connection, it's a great way to meet new people while enjoying nature.

○ If you're a homebody, force yourself to get out of the house at least once a week and into a target-rich environment that suits your personality. Whether it's an independent film festival, a gourmet cooking class, or a singles event, you owe it to yourself and your *happily ever after* future to get out of the house and back in the game. It may feel uncomfortable at first, but I promise you it gets easier!

○ If you're a single parent, join a single parent support group, or look for single parent-oriented singles events to attend.

Take a Crash Course in Online Dating

Be honest—does the idea of online dating excite you or send you running for cover? Whether this is your first foray into the world of cyber-romance, or online dating has been part of your savvy single arsenal off and on for the past decade, or a vague but less-than-satisfactory memory of past online dating experiences taints your feelings on the subject, it's time to wipe the slate clean and embrace online dating for what it really is—practice. And you know what they say, practice makes perfect. So, as you enroll in Single U, online dating is going to be an important part of your curriculum. Here's why:

1. Online dating allows you to see that at any given time there are plenty of single people out there (having options is a good thing!).

2. Online dating offers 24/7 access to potential partner profiles (so you can browse and contact people when it's convenient for you).

3. With so many online options you can easily date more than one person at a time, which takes the pressure off any single encounter (and lets you just have fun!).

4. Online dating gives you plenty of practice at defining and refining your personal dating style.

5. Online dating allows you to get to know someone virtually first before meeting them in person (giving you plenty of time to decide if you want to pursue a first date or cut your losses and move on).

Now that you know some of the perks of online dating, you should give it a try—even if it's just for fun! If you're not ready to date yet (and that's perfectly fine), do an online search for free dating sites just to start browsing. And remember those saucy pics you had taken after your makeover? Upload them to your dating site of choice, create a quick and cute online profile, and start perusing potential partners. In fact, invite your friends over to help create your flirty profile. And don't worry. Just because you create an online dating profile doesn't mean you have to go out with anyone just yet. That's the beauty of cyberdating—you decide who you want to date and when. For now, just enjoy lurking and reading people's profiles.

BREAKUP RECOVERY TIP

℞ Talk to Strangers

Ready to get back out there? It's time to get comfortable talking to strangers. Every day for thirty days, strike up a conversation with a member of the opposite sex you don't know. You can do this in line at Starbucks, at the Genius Bar in the Apple Store, or while waiting for your car to be serviced. The purpose of this exercise is not necessarily to score a date. It's to illustrate the idea that there are men everywhere and it's up to you to get comfortable talking to them. Once you do, charming that cutie you've been eyeing for weeks at your acupuncturist's office won't be so scary. Good luck!

Enroll in Other Singles Events/Options

In addition to online dating, there are plenty of other singles events you should consider. After all, you don't want to put all of your dating eggs in one basket, do you? In an effort to put yourself out there and regularly practice meeting your fellow singles, you may want to consider any or all of the following options:

o Attend in-person singles events like speed dating, singles mixers.

o Let your friends know when you're ready to get back out on the dating scene in case they want to set you up with someone or organize a group singles event.

- Investigate professional matchmaking services.
- Hire a relationship coach for ongoing dating tips, techniques, and tools.
- Go on a singles-oriented vacation like a cruise or guided international tour.

Rebounding 101

Okay, it's time to talk about something you've probably already considered during the last two and a half weeks, but (let's hope) haven't acted on yet. I'm talking about rebounding. While it's not a recommended Single U activity, it may be a course you're contemplating. That's why it's part of this chapter. If you're going to participate, you should have all the facts.

First, let's define rebounding. The good news is it doesn't necessarily mean jumping into bed with someone. Rebounding can be as simple as flirting with a cute stranger (see previous section), or as harmless as exchanging a few passionate kisses with someone new. However, if you're a woman of extremes, your rebound may end up going all the way. With this in mind, let's review the pros and cons. Yes, rebounding can make you feel sexy, desirable, and wanted. Plus, knowing that your ex wasn't the last man to touch you or kiss you may feel incredibly empowering. However, rebounding also has a downside. It can fill you with regret, make you question your sanity, or send you running back to your ex if the rebound was less than satisfying. And that's a definite no-no. Still, if you're intent on rebounding, be sure to have your Boo-Hoo Crew

on speed dial in case of an emotional meltdown, and adhere to the following dos and don'ts:

DO: Try to keep your rebound as harmless as possible (flirting and kissing only). Keep in mind that your rebound is just a rebound (not a new relationship), and give yourself permission to change your mind if things get too intense.

DON'T: Rebound with someone from work (it'll just add more drama to your life), tell your ex about the rebound, talk about your ex during the rebound, or go home with a complete stranger.

I hope you'll just say no to rebounding. I think it's just far too confusing at this stage in your recovery. Besides, there will be plenty of time for kissing cuties in your *happily ever after* future.

 Chapter *Check-In*

Only you will know when it's time to get back out there and start dating again. Don't rush your recovery or force your feelings. However, you also don't want to get so comfortable in your recovery cocoon that you never break free and become that beautiful butterfly. Trust that your gut will let you know when your heart has sufficiently healed and is open to dating again. At that time, return to this chapter, review the information, and get your fabulous flirt on!

Now, as an added bonus for being such a recovery rock star, I invite you to visit my website and download a free forty-five-minute MP3 titled "26 Secrets Successful Singles Know." If you incorporate just one of these secrets every week, you'll have six months' worth of valuable information—for free! Here's the webpage to go to for your free download: *www.LisaSteadman.com/SingleSecrets*. Class dismissed!

worksheet 1
put yourself in target-rich environments

Even if you're not ready to get back out there just yet, make a list of at least five target-rich environments here. When you're ready, regularly get yourself out there!

DATE _____

_____

_____

_____

_____

_____

_____

_____

_____

_____

_____

_____

worksheet 2
create your online dating profile

Just for fun, create your online dating profile. Review and revise until you're satisfied. Ask your friends for their input if needed. Then post it on your dating site of choice and have fun perusing the possibilities!

DATE _____

_____

_____

_____

_____

_____

_____

_____

_____

_____

_____

_____

_____

worksheet 3
identify and reframe your bad love habits

Make a list of any limiting beliefs you currently hold on to about love and relationships. Then rewrite those beliefs to embrace more positive ones.

Repeat your new belief system every morning and every night for thirty days. For more info on breaking free of limiting relationship beliefs, visit *www .BadLoveNoMore.com*.

DATE _____

Old Belief: _____

_____

New Belief: _____

_____

Old Belief: _____

_____

New Belief: _____

_____

Old Belief: _____

_____

New Belief: _____

_____

DAY 20
an EX
marks the plot

Today, I feel . . .

_____

_____

_____

There have probably been many times during your recovery when you've questioned your ability to merely survive the breakup. There have most likely been times when you believed that your fabulousness left with your ex (*so* not true!), but how are you feeling now? As you continue moving on, there will definitely be temptation to pick up the phone and dial your ex's digits even though you know it's the last thing you should do. But, as many bad times as there have been and may still be because of *what's his name*, today's the day to acknowledge the good in him. It's time to honor the memory of the two of you and to count the lessons learned as you heal and move on from here. Don't worry, you can hate your ex *and* still give thanks that he once was the most important person in your life.

Perform an Emotional Ex-orcism

If the idea of celebrating your ex or your relationship freaks you out or has you worried that you'll run back to him, don't skip this chapter. That's not going to happen. You've come too far to turn back now, even if you wanted to just for a minute. What you'll discover here is just as important to your recovery as all the other chapters have been. So, summon that inner strength and keep reading. It's time to ex-cavate your ex's memory in hopes of celebrating the good, giving up the ghosts of the bad, and facing the oh-so ugly.

Have an Ex-it Strategy

With just one more day left in this journey together, you may have some hesitation about how to handle feelings for your ex moving forward. The truth is it's okay to still have feelings for him. Three weeks is not a long time. And even with all the progress you've made, you're human. A part of you probably still loves, misses, or thinks about him from time to time. Or all the time. Or better yet—none of the time! That's part of the healing process. Let yourself feel whatever you feel for your ex. But at the same time, acknowledge that he is no longer a part of your life, and for that reason, along with so many others, you should not reach out and reconnect. Nor should you be open to your ex reconnecting. And chances are good that he will.

See, ex-boyfriends have a sixth sense about when their ex-girlfriends are getting over them. Although he may not want you back, he doesn't necessarily want you moving on without him either. As romantic as that may sound (trust me, it's not!), it's poisonous to your recovery. So, if and when you see your ex's digits on your cell phone, discover a string of flirty text messages he sent you late one night, notice an influx of e-mail in your inbox, or worse, you run into your ex while you're out and about, know that it's no accident. Understand that his tiny, little, overinflated ego is feeling bruised and these chance encounters are actually preplanned.

Again, take your ego out of the equation, and instead focus on your continued recovery. Screen his call, delete his e-mail, and sidestep any in-person encounters. You can only do better when you know better. And after all the work you've done, you definitely know better!

Identify the Good

Now that you've committed to keeping your ex out of your recovery moving forward, you can focus on learning some valuable lessons from the relationship. Start by asking yourself what it was about your relationship that you cherished. Not only that, I want you to think about the traits and

qualities your ex possessed that you may actually want in a future partner. Keep in mind that acknowledging these good qualities does not mean you should put your ex on a pedestal. Think of it a relationship autopsy. Your life with *what's his name* is dead and gone with no chance of resuscitation. All you're doing today is undergoing an emotional autopsy in hopes of learning from what was right as well as what went wrong. Brainstorm about what it was that you cherished about your ex or your relationship that you may want in a future relationship and continue writing at the end of the chapter.

TRAITS AND QUALITIES I CHERISHED ABOUT MY EX AND OUR RELATIONSHIP:

1. I really appreciated my ex's easy-going nature.
2. When the relationship was good, we had a lot of fun together.
3. I admired my ex's close relationship with his family.
4. My ex was a great kisser.
5. My ex was very supportive of me.

6. _____

   _____

7. _____

   _____

Again, don't use this list as an excuse to pick up the phone and call *what's his name*. The goal of this exercise is to excavate any positive traits and qualities from your buried relationship in the hope of resurrecting them in a future relationship with someone better suited for you. By knowing what you value, you're better able to attract it down the road.

Embrace the Bad and/or Ugly

Your next order of business is to make a list of the traits and qualities your ex *didn't* have but that you'd like to find in a future partner. (See, I told you this chapter wouldn't send you running back to your ex—and you doubted me.) Give yourself permission to create your dream vision of your perfect partner, being as specific as possible. Consider the examples below or add your own to get started on Worksheet 1.

Remember, there are no limits to what is possible, so dream—you guessed it—B-I-G! Plus, by dreaming big, you once again engage the law of attraction and bring your perfect partner that much closer to your reality.

Identify the Lessons You've Learned

Now, I want you to think about what life lessons you might be learning as a result of the breakup. It may be too soon to have the benefit of hindsight, but if you do, give this exercise a try. What, if anything, have you learned about yourself or the relationship that is valuable to your *happily ever after* future? If you need inspiration, the following are examples or you can brainstorm for Worksheet 2 here.

TRAITS AND QUALITIES MY EX DID NOT POSSESS BUT THAT I'D LIKE TO FIND IN MY PERFECT PARTNER:

1. Has strong family values / wants to start a family with me
2. Loves his job, but doesn't live for it
3. Doesn't have to make tons of money, but should live well within his means
4. Doesn't take himself or life too seriously
5. Knows who he is and is comfortable in his own skin

6. _____

7. _____

VALUABLE LESSONS I'VE LEARNED, THANKS TO MY RELATIONSHIP AND/OR THE BREAKUP:

1. From now on, I will always listen to my gut in relationships.
2. I will never settle for less than I deserve.
3. I now know how I want to be treated by my perfect partner.
4. In the future, I will not put up with abusive, demeaning, bad behavior.
5. Learning to love myself will make it so much easier to find a partner who can love me.

6. _____

7. _____

It's important to record whatever insights you've discovered since the breakup happened. In doing so, you create a road map for future healthy, happy, and whole relationships. Again, if it's too soon, return to this exercise as you learn your valuable breakup lessons in the future.

Assess Your Emotional Baggage

Yesterday you got a crash course in being single. Although you may be far from ready to start dating again, it's important to assess how much emotional baggage you're currently carrying and if you need to dump any of it before you can move on. Of course, emotional baggage is different from the valuable lessons you're learning in your recovery. While it's essential to learn your lessons from past relationships and carry that wisdom and knowledge into your future, holding on to unnecessary emotional baggage is detrimental to your future relationship success. So how do you tell the difference between unnecessary emotional baggage and the valuable lessons you've learned? The following scenarios illustrate the not-so-subtle differences. Review them and see which category you fall into.

You may have emotional baggage if:

o Your emotional walls are so high that no one can get in—or out.
o Every guy you meet reminds you of your ex (in all the bad ways).
o You quickly find fault with any guy who shows any sign of interest in you.
o If someone in your life doesn't call when they say they're going to, is late once or twice, or forgets something important to you, you flip out, shut them out, or shut down.

You may be wisely applying lessons learned if:

o You give potential dates the benefit of the doubt, but only if no other red flags are present.
o When someone's bad behavior repeatedly reminds you of your ex's bad behavior, you calmly but quickly call them on it.
o You pay attention to a potential date's actions as well as their words, and when they don't match, you decide whether to stay or go.
o You respect yourself and expect that others will treat you with respect (if they don't, you're gone).

Here's another distinction to make between the two: Lessons learned allow you to move forward in life with a healthy attitude, while excess emotional baggage can hold you back, bring you down, and keep you from experiencing real relationships in the future. You owe it to yourself to identify which category you fall into and, if needed, dump that excess baggage!

 Chapter *Check-In*

Today, you performed an emotional autopsy on your ex and your relationship, assessed your emotional baggage, and held yourself accountable for your healing heart. Be honest—are you still in post-breakup pain? If so, don't be afraid to admit it. Everybody's recovery is different. If you're still hurting as you heal, that's perfectly natural. However, to make sure your pain and suffering don't become unnecessarily prolonged afflictions, I want you to do yourself a favor. Tonight, get out your recovery challenge calendar and flip to a date in the future that you feel comfortable claiming as an end date for your post-breakup pain. It can be next week, next month, or the end of the year. It can even be sometime next year if you think it'll take that long. Only you can know for sure how long your suffering should last. I'll just give you my professional opinion. Don't let it last any longer than it has to! That's what the end date is for—so that if you're still experiencing a lot of heartbreak, you can allow for additional recovery time without prolonging the pain. There's a very fine line between giving yourself permission to grieve and basking in your post-breakup pain like a masochist. I'm going to ask you to hold yourself accountable, and trust that you will not extend the grieving process any longer than necessary.

worksheet 1
ex-cavate the relationship

To improve your chances of relationship success in the future, first identify the traits and qualities you appreciate about your ex and the relationship you had together. Then, identify the traits and qualities your ex lacked but that you'd like to find in your perfect partner.

DATE _____

Traits and qualities I cherished about my ex and our relationship:

_____

_____

_____

_____

_____

_____

_____

_____

_____

_____

Traits and qualities my ex did not possess that I'd like to find in my perfect partner:

_____

_____

_____

_____

_____

_____

_____

_____

_____

_____

_____

_____

_____

_____

_____

_____

worksheet 2
identify lessons learned

If you're ready, identify the lessons you're learning from your relationship with your ex and/or the breakup itself. If it's too soon, return to this page as the lessons reveal themselves to you in the future.

DATE _____

Valuable lessons I've learned, thanks to my relationship and/or breakup:

_____

_____

_____

_____

_____

_____

_____

_____

_____

_____

_____

_____

DAY 21
celebrate
your SUCCESS

Congratulations! Welcome to the final day in your twenty-one-day recovery. You did it! Not only did you survive your breakup, but you're now ready and well equipped to thrive. How do you feel today? Even if you only did a portion of the work involved and some of the worksheets included in this book, you've still taken monumental strides toward healing and moving on from your breakup. And now it's time to celebrate! Not only should you throw yourself a Movin' On party in the near future, but you should definitely take some time today to acknowledge, honor, and celebrate your commitment to your recovery. So come on, Party Girl. Let the festivities begin!

Throw a Movin' On Party

Okay, rock star. All that hard work you've been doing is starting to pay off. And to celebrate, today or in the near future, you deserve to throw your-self a super fab Movin' On party. Invite all of your friends who helped you through the breakup, most especially your Boo-Hoo Crew. In fact, call them right now and let them know that they've been promoted to Woo-Hoo Crew status. That's right—now that you're moving on to life after the breakup, so is your Boo-Hoo Crew. It's time to thank them for their commitment to your recovery and toast to your bright futures!

Of course, how you choose to celebrate is up to you. You may decide to throw a huge party, invite everyone you know, and dance till dawn. Or you may opt for a low-key affair at your fave restaurant with your closest friends. Or you may choose to make your soirée super small, inviting only your Woo-Hoo Crew. Remember, the point of your Movin' On party is to celebrate your progress in the manner and style that suits your wants and needs. In other words, just have fun!

Who will you invite to your Movin' On party?

_____   _____

_____   _____

_____   _____

_____   _____

_____   _____

_____   _____

_____   _____

Movin' On Party Planning Dos and Don'ts

Since the purpose of the fabulous festivities is to celebrate moving on, you'll want to leave talk of your ex and your relationship behind. The following are some simple Movin' On party dos and don'ts:

DO: Invite only your loving and supportive friends, focus on your fab future, and just have fun!

DON'T: Invite people who will dish party details with your ex, spend the entire night talking about your ex, or use the party as an excuse to contact your ex.

Write a Letter to Your Future Self

Even with all the progress you've made, you may still have questions about where to go from here. You may even feel uncertain how to embody that fab future self you've been writing about or how to fully embrace the bright future I've been talking about throughout the second half of this book. While I definitely don't plan on leaving you hanging (See the "What Now?" section following this chapter), I also want to empower you to leave behind as much *boo-hoo* as possible so you can enjoy a whole lot of *Woo-hoo* moving forward. To get you started on that *Woo-hoo* journey, I invite you to write a letter to your future self (see the worksheet at the end of the chapter). In your letter, feel free to address where you are emotionally right this second, as well as ask any questions. Be sure to include any doubts, fears, or worries that you're experiencing along with resolutions you'd like your future self to have experienced by the time she reads the letter. Your letter may go something like the following:

Dear Future Me,

How are you? I hope this letter finds you well. As I'm writing, I'm just finishing up our 21-day breakup recovery program. We've definitely come a long way and learned a lot of amazing lessons! For example, I now know that I'm much stronger than I ever realized before. And, while it was hard to walk away from a relationship with what's his name, I do believe that our future is going to be so much better without him. I hope that by the time you read this, you're completely moved into your new home, have thrown yourself a fabulous house-warming party, and have made going to the gym a priority again.

Right now, I still really miss Mr. Ex. And I'm pretty hurt by all those awful things he said and did. To be honest, I can't imagine ever falling in love again. As you read this, I hope you miss him less or better yet, not at all. He's so not worth our time or energy! I also hope you're starting to believe that love can happen for us at some point in the future. I'd like to think we deserve to meet somebody pretty amazing. What do you think?

Well, that's all for now. I love you very much and I'm so proud of everything we've been through.

xoxo,

Lisa

190

Create Accountability Contract 2

I can't believe I'm saying this, but I have one final activity for you to do during your twenty-one-day recovery. Just one more and you're done! Are you ready for it? Your final assignment is to create an accountability contract for your healing heart. This was an exercise I originally created for the beginning of Part Two of my first book. My readers loved it! In fact, it was so successful that I now encourage anyone I coach to create their very own accountability contract, regardless of where they are on the journey from *boo-hoo* to *Woo-hoo!*

So, in honor of your healing heart and your *happily ever after* future, I invite you to create an accountability contract of your own. By creating and signing your accountability contract (see the worksheet at the end of the chapter), you promise to never again give your heart away foolishly, to be a wise judge of character when it comes to future relationships, and to practice both patience and prudence in choosing the person you give your heart to next.

The following is the sample accountability contract from my first book. Feel free to borrow from it or add your own ideas to create your contract at the end of the chapter.

I, _____,
being of sound mind and healed heart, promise to be a worthy keeper of my healed heart. As the keeper of my healed heart, I agree to the following:

o I will never again give my heart to anyone who is undeserving of it.
o I will pay attention to relationship red flags as they are revealed to me.

o When I'm ready, I trust myself to exercise excellent judgment in selecting a suitable candidate to fall in love with (one who is capable of loving me on the same level).
o In the meantime, I trust myself to date (when I'm ready) and to be open to the possibilities.
o I am healthy and strong enough to endure any dating disappointments that happen along the way, and I will be able to differentiate those disappointments from actual heartbreak.
o I will not let any baggage from the past affect my future relationships. In fact, I have checked all unnecessary baggage and am now traveling with nothing more than a compact backpack full of lessons learned.
o I dedicate myself wholeheartedly to living and loving my life as it is right now (and fixing the things that no longer work, so I can live and love my life even more).
o I recognize that having failed relationships in the past does not make me a failure at love.
o I am now free to welcome (at my discretion) healthy, happy, whole love into my life!

Signed: _____

Date: _____

 ## Chapter *Check-In*

Welcome to your very last Chapter Check-In. I hope you took the time today to celebrate your numerous successes along this journey. You've done incredible work, and I am so proud of you. Whether you know it or not, your future is already here and it's so bright and beautiful! To fully heal and move on, be sure to plan and throw the most amazing Movin' On party for yourself—and from here on out, practice plenty of self-nurturing activities. Whatever you do, do not skip over the task of drafting your own accountability contract. Your healing heart is counting on you! In creating this contract, you start the next phase of your recovery. But don't worry. Even without my guidance, you're still in excellent hands—yours! That's right. You are now ready to continue this journey alone. When in doubt, review the chapters and worksheets in this book. And if there's a particular section that you're struggling with, definitely review it regularly and do the worksheets again.

Finally, thank you. It has been my absolute pleasure to take you on this journey. I invite you to continue our journey together by visiting *www.Lisa Steadman.com*. There, I'm more than happy to continue guiding you toward your fab *Woo-hoo!* future. In the meantime, I wish you much love, happiness, and continued healing.

worksheet 1
plan your movin' on party

Use the space here to start planning your party.
Brainstorm the guest list, menu, beverages, loca-
tion, music, etc. Remember—this is your bash.
Make it fun!

DATE _____

_____

_____

_____

_____

_____

_____

_____

_____

_____

_____

worksheet 1
*plan your movin' on party—*continued

_____

_____

_____

_____

_____

_____

_____

_____

_____

_____

_____

_____

_____

_____

_____

_____

_____

_____

worksheet 2
write your future self a letter

What would you like to say to your future self? Be
sure to include any fears, worries, uncertainties as
well as any hopes, dreams, and resolutions you'd
like to experience between now and the time your
future self reads the letter. Then include a date to
read the letter, mark your calendar, and return to
this page at that future date.

DATE _____

_____

_____

_____

_____

_____

_____

_____

_____

_____

_____

_____

_____

worksheet 2
write your future self a letter—continued

_____

_____

_____

_____

_____

_____

_____

_____

_____

_____

_____

_____

_____

_____

_____

_____

_____

_____

worksheet 3
create an accountability contract

As the keeper of your healing heart, you owe it to your recovery to create and sign an accountability contract. Feel free to borrow from the one printed on page 191 or create your very own here.

DATE _____

_____

_____

_____

_____

_____

_____

_____

_____

_____

_____

_____

recovery challenge

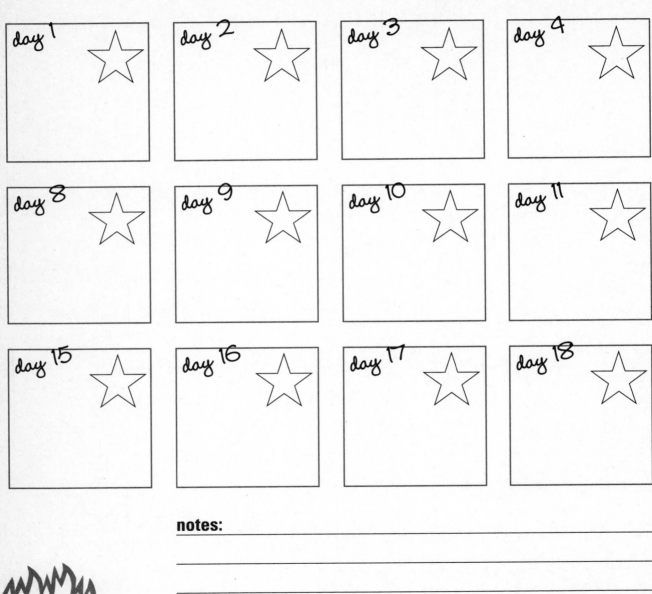

day 1 ⭐

day 2 ⭐

day 3 ⭐

day 4 ⭐

day 8 ⭐

day 9 ⭐

day 10 ⭐

day 11 ⭐

day 15 ⭐

day 16 ⭐

day 17 ⭐

day 18 ⭐

notes: _____
_____
_____
_____
_____

198

Make this a gold-star day! Use this calendar on your road to heartbreak recovery and go from sad to FAB in three short weeks!

 day 5

 day 6

 day 7

 day 12

 day 13

 day 14

 day 19

 day 20

 day 21

it's a
BREAKUP not a
BREAKDOWN
WORKBOOK

_____

_____

_____

_____

_____

what now?

Hi again. If you're reading this, it means you got to the end of the book and still want more information. You didn't really think I'd leave you hanging, did you? Not after all the awesome work you've done. Okay, so you want more? Throughout the book, I've given you plenty of opportunities to go to my website and access free information. If you're like me, your time online is already jam-packed full of places to go and things to do. What if I told you I created one location for you to access everything I promised you'd find on my website? How much easier would that make your life and your recovery? The answer is very! So the next time you're online, visit *www.LisaSteadman.com/workbookrockstar*. There, you'll find all the tips, tools, and freebies previously mentioned in the book. Enjoy!

index

about the author

Internationally known as The Relationship Journalist™, Lisa Steadman is an author, speaker, and success coach dedicated to helping women move away from the pain of the past and into their brilliant futures. She regularly contributes to the media, including appearances on *The Today Show*, *The Tyra Banks Show*, Playboy Radio, and New Zealand's *Good Morning*. Lisa lives in Southern California with her husband, whom she met and married after successfully surviving and thriving following her Big Breakup. She can be found at LisaSteadman.com.

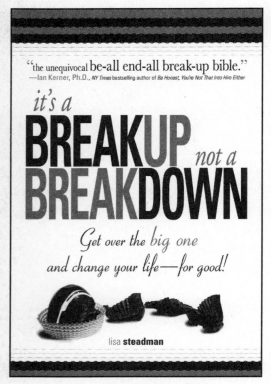

"the unequivocal be-all end-all break-up bible."
—Ian Kerner, Ph.D., *NY Times* bestselling author of *Be Honest, You're Not That Into Him Either*

it's a
BREAKUP *not a*
BREAKDOWN

*Get over the big one
and change your life—for good!*

lisa **steadman**

Trade Paperback, $14.95
ISBN 10: 1-59869-172-4
ISBN 13: 978-1-59869-172-6

REINVENT YOUR BREAKUP...
and your life!

AVAILABLE WHEREVER BOOKS ARE SOLD!
Or visit us at *www.adamsmediastore.com* or call 1-800-258-0929.